REFORMATION AND REVIVAL

THE Solution
for the Middle East Conflict?

Dr. Al Nucciarone

Reformation and Revival: The Solution for the Middle East Conflict?

ISBN 978-965-7542-04-0

Photos and Illustrations: Internet.

Editing and Lay-out:
Petra van der Zande, Tsur Tsina Publications, Jerusalem, Israel.

Order information:

Email: nucciaro@aol.com

Or via www.Lulu.com

Table of Contents

Acknowledgements

I would like to thank the Lord for my wife Billie, who has encouraged me and has added her writing flair.

I am so grateful for our beloved sister in the Lord, Petra van der Zande for her example, encouragement and editing. She is a true inspiration.

Finally, I bless the congregation of the Jerusalem Baptist church for their love and patience.

Foreword

"If my people who are called by my Name,
humble themselves, and pray
and turn from their evil ways,
then I will hear their prayers
and heal their land".

2 Chronicles 7:14

When I was eight years old, my parents took me on a trip to
Washington, DC. that set the direction of my life, or so I thought.
When we visited the FBI building, I thought it was the coolest
place in the world - especially watching the agents at the
shooting range. We then visited the Senate Chambers and I saw
Senator John Kennedy on the floor doing some negotiations.
I was in awe. From that day on I knew I wanted to be either an
FBI agent or a politician. That meant I needed to become a
lawyer. This was my dream.

If anyone had told me then that one day I would be living in
Jerusalem preaching the Gospel, I would have said they were
crazy. God had his Way in my life and I came to know Christ as
my personal Lord and Savior at a Billy Graham Crusade on
June 25, 1970.

Within one year I knew I wanted to be in Christian work. I had
the privilege of being involved with Campus Crusade for Christ
at the University of Maryland and learned much about sharing
Christ, discipleship and having a world vision. The Lord led me to
Dallas Seminary to prepare me for the ministry and here I
became interested in world missions and church growth.

The Lord then thrust me onto the mission field where we worked in Italy, Austria, and now in Israel. My doctoral studies were in the area of church growth which led to a study of Biblical Revivals. 2 Chronicles 7:14 states: "If my people who are called by my Name, humble themselves, and pray and turn from their evil ways, then I will hear their prayers and heal their land". This became a theme of my ministry. I began to eat, sleep and drink revival and church growth.

Now that we are in Israel and in the Middle East, I believe it is time to share a message like this. The Middle East is in crisis. There is the threat of ISIS and other terrorist groups who have one objective: to dominate the world and get rid of Christians, Jews, and Muslims who do not believe exactly as they do.

Brother Andrew stated that the challenge for the church in the 20th century was Communism, but that in the 21st century it is Islam. How do we deal with this challenge? How can we have real peace in the Middle East.? There is only one solution: the Gospel of Jesus Christ and a revived church that demonstrates the love of Christ.

I wrote this book to share a Biblical solution to the challenges we face here in the Middle East and the world. May the Lord use it for His glory.

Dr. Al Nucciarone
Jerusalem, June 2015

CHAPTER 1

REFORMATION AND REVIVAL TODAY

Throughout the history of the Christian church there has never been a more desperate and perilous time than the one we live in today. Truly, the last days are upon us. Jesus spoke about this time in Matthew 24 when He talked about the signs of His coming. He said there would be wars, earthquakes, famines, and false prophets and that the Gospel would be preached in the whole world. According to the Bible, the "latter days" is the time period between the two comings of Christ. The apostle Paul also spoke about this time in his letter to Timothy. He said in 1 Timothy 4 that men will fall from the faith and be deceived by doctrines of demons, and that false religions will permeate the world. In 2 Timothy 3, Paul describes a world in which there will be wars, hatred, violence, crime, disobedience to parents and the rise of false religions.

Rocket Launchers in the Gaza Strip

My wife and I have been living in Israel for the past seven years and we have faced and continue to face many of these things daily. There are periodic terrorist attacks on the streets and when skirmishes escalate, rockets fall from Gaza, Lebanon and Syria.

Israel lives with the constant specter of a nuclear attack by Iran. In spite of all the attempts at bridging peoples and narratives and all the conferences held on the subject, there is no peace in the Middle East.

When we watch the news on T.V. we realize that the whole world is in turmoil and facing the things described as characteristic of the last days.

The Bible tells us exactly where the problem lies in all this unrest. Jeremiah says, "The heart is desperately wicked, who can understand it." The problem causing the unrest in the world is the sinful heart of man. In James 4, the apostle asked, "What causes fights and quarrels among you?" And the answer? "Don't they come from your desires that battle within you? You want something but don't get it. You kill and covet, but you cannot have what you want. You quarrel and fight."

So, what is the solution? The heart of man must be changed.

Changed from within

How can this be done? There is only one solution. Men's hearts must be changed from within through the power and grace of Jesus Christ. Peace on the earth will ultimately occur when Jesus comes. In the meantime we are to preach the Prince of Peace that we may be reconciled to God and to each other. What we need is a spiritual revival from our Sovereign God. This is the real need in the Middle East and the world. It starts with each one of us.

The times we live in now are similar to the times of King Hezekiah, one of the good kings of Judah. In those days there was war and idolatry in the land. God raised up two men to bring the nation back to God, and the country experienced true revival.

We need to learn from these men - Isaiah the prophet, and King Hezekiah. We need men and women today who will lead people to repentance and obedience to God, thus ushering in revival. Men and women like Billy Graham, Billy Sunday, Beth Moore, Lottie Moon and Anne Graham Lotz.

Billie Sunday

Anne Graham Lotz

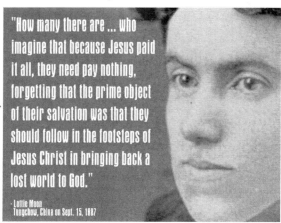

"How many there are ... who imagine that because Jesus paid it all, they need pay nothing, forgetting that the prime object of their salvation was that they should follow in the footsteps of Jesus Christ in bringing back a lost world to God."

- Lottie Moon
Tungchou, China on Sept. 15, 1887

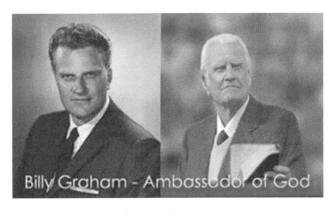

Billy Graham - Ambassador of God

Quotes by Billy Graham

◊ Comfort and prosperity have never enriched the world as much as adversity has.

◊ When wealth is lost, nothing is lost; when health is lost, something is lost; when character is lost, all is lost.

◊ There is nothing wrong with men possessing riches. The wrong comes when riches possess men.

◊ Being a Christian is more than just an instantaneous conversion; it is like a daily process whereby you grow to be more and more like Christ.

◊ No man ever loved like Jesus. He taught the blind to see and the dumb to speak. He died on the cross to save us. He bore our sins. And now God says, Because He did, I can forgive you.

◊ My home is in Heaven. I'm just traveling through this world.

CHAPTER 2

INTRODUCING HEZEKIAH

I became a believer in Jesus at a Billy Graham Crusade on June 15, 1970 in New York City. As Billy Graham is my spiritual father, it is always a joy for me to go through the museum in Wheaton, Illinois, that commemorates his life and is dedicated

Billy Graham during a Crusade

to revival and evangelism. Certainly Dr. Graham has been used of God in this generation to call people back to Him. Dr. Graham has been a catalyst for worldwide revival.

He describes the condition of the world with its idolatry, drug use, marital decadence, and general immorality. He calls for repentance, which means a turning from sin to God, and preaches Christ as the only mediator between God and man and as the one who died to pay the penalty for our sin. The preaching of this message and its application to the lives of people has changed lives, churches, and societies.

It is a well-known fact that Billy Graham has also had an influence on American presidents and world leaders with, and for whom, he has prayed.

Billy Graham with JF Kennedy

Something similar happened in the Old Testament in the history of Israel. In those days, God used a man similar to Billy Graham to preach a message of repentance and faith in God. This man also had an influence on a political leader. That man was the prophet Isaiah. He was raised up by God to preach to the nation of Israel and in particular to the kings of Judah. Those were days of apostasy and idol worship. God was about to judge Israel by bringing another nation against them. The leader that Isaiah influenced was King Hezekiah. There is a short synopsis of his reign in 2 Kings 18:1-8, and several chapters in Isaiah also speak of the prophet's ministry to Hezekiah and to his father Ahaz.

---

2 Kings 18:1-8 Holman Bible

"In the third year of Israel's King Hoshea son of Elah, Hezekiah son of Ahaz became king of Judah. He was 25 years old when he became king and reigned 29 years in Jerusalem. His mother's name was Abi daughter of Zechariah. He did what was right in the LORD's sight just as his ancestor David had done. He removed the high places, shattered the pillars, and cut down the Asherah poles. He broke into pieces the bronze snake that Moses made, for the Israelites burned incense to it up to that time. He called it Nehushtan. Hezekiah trusted in the LORD God of Israel; not one of the kings of Judah was like him, either him or after him. He remained faithful to Yahweh not turning from following Him but kept the commands the LORD had commanded Moses. The LORD was with him, and wherever he went he prospered. He rebelled against the king of Assyria and did not serve him. He defeated the Philistines as far as Gaza and its borders, from watchtower to fortified city."

Hezekiah was born into an idolatrous family. His father, King Ahaz, was probably the worst king of Judah. He even sacrificed

his child to the Canaanite god, Moloch. God chose and prepared Isaiah for such a time as that. In fact, the year Hezekiah was born was the very year Isaiah received his call from God recounted in Isaiah 6. We learn in 2 Kings 18 that Hezekiah was 25 years old when he began to reign in Judah. He was young and at that time very open to new ideas—the right time to meet Isaiah. After studying

The Prophet Isaiah

these passages it appears to me that Isaiah became Hezekiah's mentor and was used by God to lead Hezekiah to the Lord through his own testimony (Isaiah 6). Like Hezekiah, we need mentors, older men and women who can encourage us, teach us, rebuke us, if needed, and love us.

Without the guidance and accountability a mentor can offer, we can deviate from the Truth and God's plan for our lives.

Evan Roberts, a 17 year old Welsh man, was used by God to bring revival to Wales, sharing one powerful message: "Bend me Lord Jesus."

God blessed him and used him greatly. However, as years went by, Evan became somewhat eccentric and tended toward extremism.

Evan Roberts

Mr. Richard Owen Roberts, a great writer on revivals, explains that Mr. Roberts might not have gone astray if he had sought guidance from a wiser, older mentor who could have kept him balanced.

In this book, I would like to explore the revival and reformation principles that are exemplified in the life and ministry of King Hezekiah and encouraged by the prophet Isaiah. Let us remember that all that we see in his life came as a result of the grace of God and the ministry of the prophet.

The principles for revival are:

1. A passion for God
2. Purging of sin and idolatry
3. Putting into practice the Word of God
4. Provision for Sin
5. Preaching of repentance and God's provision for sin.
6. Praise and worship of our Almighty God.
7. Prayer - the greatest force on earth.

In the following chapters, I will dive into each of these principles.

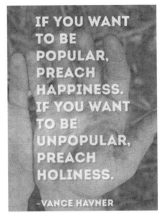

IF YOU WANT TO BE POPULAR, PREACH HAPPINESS. IF YOU WANT TO BE UNPOPULAR, PREACH HOLINESS.

-VANCE HAVNER

CHAPTER 3

A PASSION FOR GOD

The first principle for revival is the need to have a passion for God. We read in 2 Kings 18 that Hezekiah did right before the Lord. This was in complete contrast to his father who did evil in the eyes of God and disallowed temple worship and erected high places and idols to worship foreign gods. Hezekiah was righteous in God's eyes because his heart was right before God. God ignited a love and passion in Hezekiah's heart. How did He do this? We read in Isaiah 6 of God's call upon the life of Isaiah the prophet. I believe that Isaiah was able to share his testimony - a great demonstration of the Gospel of Jesus Christ. Many consider the book of Isaiah to be a prophetic gospel message.

In Isaiah 6, Isaiah receives a vision of God. He sees the Lord on the throne high and lifted up. He sees the holiness of God, his own sinfulness becoming very apparent. This new understanding, of who God was, His exaltation and greatness, and His holiness, inspired in Isaiah a passion for God. If we want a passion for God, we, too, need to understand who God is. We need to try to understand His qualities, and character, and grasp His holiness and greatness. Let's take a look at this great God.

Our All-Seeing God

It is easy to fool ourselves or our friends and family into thinking that we truly desire revival. But God knows our hearts. Our God is a sovereign, all seeing, and all knowing God. Nothing escapes His eye. We may hide things from our friends. We may hide things from our wife and children. But, we cannot hide anything from God. Psalm 139 says, "Where can I go from Thy presence, where can I flee from thy spirit?" Nowhere.

Jonah tried to run away

Jonah thought he could escape from the presence of God. God had commanded him to go and preach to the Ninevites who were Israel's enemies. However, Jonah wanted them to be judged. He did not want them to hear God's message— "repent and be forgiven." So he ran away. He learned his lesson that he could not hide from an all seeing, all knowing God the hard way.

I was recently reminded of God's omnipresence and omniscience at a store in Jerusalem. Israel is a country known for its sophisticated security and surveillance systems. While I was waiting to be served at the cellphone store near my home, I went to the men's room and put my car keys on the sink. I left the restroom in a rush, thinking I might have missed my number being called. Two hours later after finish-ing up with the sales associate, I realized that I couldn't find my keys. I rushed to the men's room, thinking they might still be on the sink, but the keys were not there. Next I asked the custodian if he had seen the keys but he had not seen them. The building manager noticed my predicament, and he motioned for me to follow him into his office where he had a video screen displaying images recorded by cameras installed all around the building. He replayed the recordings close to the restroom and asked me what time I had been there. To my surprise we saw me coming out of the restroom with the keys in my right hand.

The building manager and I went back into the store to look for the keys but could not find them. Finally, he led me to the receptionist. To my relief, my keys were lying on her desk. I was so relieved I gave the manager a big hug. It reminded me that we can hide things from our friends, family, and even from Israeli security, but we cannot hide anything from God.

Are we really seeking revival, praying for it, willing to strive for it and make sacrifices for it? The Lord knows.

Our Holy God

Isaiah had a vision of God who is holy. The seraphim and the cherubim proclaimed, "Holy, Holy, Holy," demonstrating the undeniable holiness of God. It means He is totally separate from His creation. He is pure and without stain. These angels both announced and protected the holiness of God. The angels each had 6 wings. Commentators tell us that the two wings covering the eyes signify humility. The two wings covering the feet represent service, and the two that enabled them to fly represent being available to go where God leads. How do we see God in his Holiness? We must go back to the Word. The Word is a reflection of the character of God. This is implied in 2 Corinthians 3:18, where Paul says we reflect the glory of the Lord as in a mirror, and that as we gaze at him through His Word we are changed from one glory to another. The Ten Commandments and the Sermon on the Mount show us the absolute holiness and righteous standards of God.

We are to reflect God's Glory

The law becomes our tutor to lead us to Christ according to Galatians 3. In Romans 3 we are told that the law reveals our sin.

As Isaiah gazed upon the Lord in His Holiness, he saw himself as unholy and unworthy, a man of unclean lips. That look upward led to a look inward. The prophet confesses," I am a man of unclean lips and I dwell among a people of unclean lips." Here the lips represent an outward expression of our heart.

The angels not only proclaimed the holiness of God, they also searched for sin and protected God's holiness. They were also used by God to apply the holy fire of God on the lips of the prophet. Isaiah received forgiveness and cleansing immediately. The burning coals represent being cleansed by fire. God not only forgives but he also puts the desire for holiness and service into our hearts. The Lord asked, "Who will go for us?" and Isaiah was compelled to proclaim, "Here I am Lord."

Catching the Holy Fire
God also touched the life of Jeremiah. God's holy fire gripped his

heart. In Jeremiah 20 the prophet shared openly with the Lord about his difficult situation. He had been beaten and put into prison and was in chains. He complained to the Lord because speaking the Word had brought him insult and reproach. He did not want to speak any more but, he couldn't stop. The Word of the Lord was in His heart like a burning fire—the fire to live and preach the judgment and mercy of God. He could not hold it in.

Jeremiah in the dungeon

18

A man once asked the great preacher, Spurgeon, how he could attract crowds like Spurgeon did. The great man of God responded saying, "Go to the middle of the square and set yourself on fire, then you will get a crowd." He was using irony to make the point that God wants to set a preacher's heart on fire and that his burning heart will attract attention.

Spurgeon preaching

We do not know exactly how the King came to know the Lord. However, it appears that the prophet Isaiah was his spiritual mentor. We can assume that Hezekiah caught the fire from Isaiah. We read in 1 Kings 18 that Hezekiah did right in the eyes of the Lord. He did right because he got right with the Lord. The Lord forgave him and gave him the holy fire to live a holy life before the Lord and encourage his people to do the same.

Our first grandchild, Claire, is going to be two years old soon. I have only seen her three times and will rarely be able to spend time with her because we don't live near her. While visiting with her family in Wheaton recently, I was thinking about how I could serve her as I see her so infrequently. At the time, I was reading a book about God's holiness by Nancy Demoss. In it she discusses the importance of personal holiness and how our holiness affects others. Similarly, Robert Murray McCheyne, the great Scottish preacher once stated that the greatest need of his congregation was his own personal holiness.

I realized then that the greatest gift I can give Claire, or my wife, my daughters or my congregation is my personal holiness.

Hezekiah was a man of God who did right because he was right with God. He gave his personal holiness to his kingdom, and this is what we must do.

"It is not so much talents that God blesses as our conformity to Christ."

Robert Murray McCheyne

CHAPTER 4

PURGING OF SIN AND IDOLATRY

When Hezekiah came to power Judah was in terrible condition. His father, Ahaz, probably the worst king of Judah, blatantly worshipped other gods. He closed the temple and built molten images dedicated to Balaam, burnt incense in the valley of Hinnom and even sacrificed his children on the altar. He burnt incense on the high places, hills and under every green tree, and finally when God punished him for these sins by sending a foreign army against him, he sinned again by asking the King of Assyria for help rather than look-

ing to God for help. 2 Chronicles 28:23 says that these sins were his downfall and the downfall of all Israel. This was the condition of Judah when Hezekiah became king. It wasn't an easy situation. But, in 1 Kings 18:4 we read that Hezekiah cleansed the land of idolatry. "He removed the high places and shattered the sacred pillars and cut down the Asherah poles." He also abolished the worship of the bronze serpent that Moses had set up years before for the people to look to

Hezekiah cleansing the Temple

and be healed. It had become an idol. Something similar is happening in Israel today. People from all over the world come here and bow down before "holy sites." Even the cross is worshipped and quite a profit is made by those selling crosses and other religious symbols.

Purifying the Temple

Second Chronicles 29 gives us more information about Hezekiah. He is described as a ruler who did right in the eyes of the Lord like his father (ancestor) David. In his first month on the job he opened the doors of the temple and repaired them. This was the first thing he did to purge the sin in the land. Next, he brought in the priests and the Levites and instructed them to consecrate themselves and the temple. They were to remove all defilement from the sanctuary. Their fathers had turned their backs on the Lord. They shut the doors, put out the lamps, and did not burn incense or bring any burnt offerings to the sanctuary. They were judged because of this. God sent them into captivity. Hezekiah tells them he intends to make a covenant with the Lord to turn away the anger of the Lord. He gives a strong challenge to the priests and Levites to devote themselves to stand before the Lord and serve Him by burning incense.

They started their work with diligence. The priests went into the temple and removed everything unclean. The Levites took these and carried them to the Kidron Valley most likely for burning. Then they reported to the King concerning their total purification of the temple. They also rededicated the original utensils and tables which had been removed by Ahaz. The priests then began their true work of sacrificing the bulls and sprinkling the blood on the altar. The goats were also slaughtered and their blood presented on the altar to make atonement for Israel.

Burnt offerings were made and the Levites began to minister to the Lord with music and song. They could sing with true joy and worship because their hearts had been cleansed.

Idolatry had its consequences in Judah. Sin reaps destruction. As a result of this idolatry, Syria and the Northern Kingdom had invaded Judah and treated them cruelly. Wars are the result of sin. James 4:1,2 teaches us this.

> *"What is the source of wars and fights among you? Don't they come from the cravings that are at war within you? You desire and do not have. You murder and covet and cannot obtain. You fight and war. You do not have because you do not ask." James 4: 1,2 Holman*

But, Hezekiah changed the course of Israel's history. His faith in God and His word constrained him to purge the nation of idolatry and sin and to follow God and His commandments whole heartedly and God's judgment was postponed.

The Ten Commandments
Hezekiah realized that Ahaz, his father, had been punished for not keeping God's commands. In 2 Chronicles 29: 6, 8-9 he said, "For our fathers were unfaithful and did what is evil in the sight of the Lord our God.... Therefore, the wrath of the Lord was on Judah and Jerusalem and He made them an object of terror, horror, and hissing as you see with your own eyes. Our fathers fell by the sword, and our sons, our daughters, and our wives are in captivity because of this." Therefore, after purging the sin, He told the people to keep God's commands.

THE TEN COMMANDMENTS

1. I AM THE LORD YOUR GOD. YOU SHALL WORSHIP THE LORD YOUR GOD AND HIM ONLY SHALL YOU SERVE.

2. YOU SHALL NOT TAKE THE NAME OF THE LORD YOUR GOD IN VAIN.

3. REMEMBER TO KEEP HOLY THE SABBATH DAY.

4. HONOR YOUR FATHER AND YOUR MOTHER.

5. YOU SHALL NOT KILL.

6. YOU SHALL NOT COMMIT ADULTERY.

7. YOU SHALL NOT STEAL.

8. YOU SHALL NOT BEAR FALSE WITNESS.

9. YOU SHALL NOT COVET YOUR NEIGHBOR'S WIFE.

10. YOU SHALL NOT COVET YOUR NEIGHBOR'S GOODS.

Today, we, as a church, are not under the Old Testament with its requirements for worshipping at the Temple or making sacrifices. But the Ten Commandments still apply. Hezekiah had knowledge of these commandments, too. These commandments are found in Exodus 20 and can generally be divided into two parts.

The first part deals with our relationship to God and the second part with our relationship to others. In the New Testament when Jesus was asked which the greatest commandment was in the Law, His response was also divided into two parts, "Love the Lord your God with all you heart, and with all your soul, and with all your mind. This is the first and greatest commandment. And the second is like it: 'Love your neighbor as yourself.'"
(Matthew 22:37-39)
So, let's looks at the Ten Commandments, starting with the first one.

Exodus 20:3 says, "You shall have no other gods before me." Then, in the next verse God explains himself more. He says we should not make any type of idol or bow down to them or worship them because God is a jealous God who punishes the children for the sins of the father to the third and fourth generation of those who hate him. But He shows love and compassion to those who love and obey Him.

Throughout its history Israel had to deal with all of the religions of the near east. Every civilization had their religion and their gods and eventually Israel fell and adopted some of these gods. King Solomon was a good king but he gave into his lust for foreign women who brought their gods with them and caused Israel to go after these strange gods.

What Jesus said About Idolatry
Jesus confronted this problem of having other gods or idols in Matthew 16 when he took his disciples up to Caesarea Philippi where there was a heathen temple built into the rock. It was dedicated to the god, Pan. There were also other gods that were worshipped there including the goddess Nymph, the goddess of sex. In the middle of that pagan temple, Jesus posed this question to his disciples: "Who do men say that I am?"
They responded with answers like Elijah and Moses. He then asked Peter, "Who do you say that I am?" Peter responded,

Pan worship in Caesarea Philippi

25

"You are the Christ, the son of the Living God," to which Jesus replied, "Upon this rock (or upon the confession that I am the Christ) I will build my church and the gates of hell shall not prevail against it."

That heathen temple area in Caesarea Philippi was known as the "gates of hell."

Jesus is saying here, "I am the Christ, the son of the Living God and am greater than these heathen gods who do not really exist."

Who are the gods that *we* worship? Is it our wallet, our job, our nation, our religious group? We can even make our spouses and our children our gods. If we desire revival, we must purge ourselves of idolatry as Hezekiah purged idolatry from the land of Israel. The Lord must be our only God and Master.

On one occasion when Jesus was in the temple and saw the way the merchants and money changers were doing their business in the temple area, he overturned their tables and said" You have made my Father's house a den of thieves." These merchants had made money their idol. But zeal for the house of God consumed Jesus.

This practice of making money from religion is still going on in the Old City of Jerusalem. Merchants sell their religious paraphernalia which become idols to pilgrims visiting the city. They make money off those who feel the need for tangible objects to which they can bow down.

What Paul said About Idolatry

The Apostle Paul also battled with false religion and idols. In Acts 17, he found himself in the majestic city of Athens which was known for its rich culture, philosophy, art, and religion and his soul was troubled. On arriving at the Areopagus, a venue for discussion and debate, he said of the Athenians that he could tell that they were a religious people

Areopagus in Athens

because of their many objects of worship. He even saw an altar to an unknown god and proclaimed to them who this unknown God was. He said that this unknown God was the Lord of heaven and that He was calling all men to repent and come to the knowledge of the Truth.

In Acts 19, Paul confronted the worship of Artemis in the city of Ephesus. Artemis was the goddess of love and was adored by many. Sexual acts at her temple were part of their religious rites. There Paul preached Christ as the only way to God and when they believed, they began to burn their idolatrous relics.

In Romans 1, writing under the inspiration of the Holy Spirit, Paul said that man is without excuse in his rejection of God. All that God has created is a testimony to man of His existence. But man has chosen to worship the created things (idols) instead of the creator.

Again in writing to the Corinthian church the apostle Paul highlights the problem of idolatry even among believers. There was a problem of those who ate food which was dedicated to idols.

Paul said that this was acceptable since God had declared all things legitimate. However, he does warn them that idolatry can be demon worship. He does say that idols are nothing, but that there are spiritual forces that can use idols to keep believers from looking to Jesus.

In Philippians 3 Paul speaks of his accomplishments and gives his pedigree. It was part of his testimony to the believers about the importance and priority that Christ must have in our lives. Paul was a Hebrew of Hebrews. He came from the tribe of Benjamin, was a Pharisee and even persecuted the church. He could have boasted in these things. They could have been his idols. However, he says that whatever was to his profit, he counted as loss for the sake of Christ. His desire was to know Christ. We can also become enamored of our titles, degrees, and certificates. They can become idols to us.
When I am waiting in a doctor's or dentist's office, I do pay attention to the diplomas on the wall for I want to make sure they went to the right schools. It gives me confidence. I do not get the same feeling when I visit a pastor's office. Sometimes they put up their certificates to impress people. I have decided to leave all my certificates at my mother-in-law's house. I remember seeing an illustrative cartoon about a pastor who had all his titles on his door, ending with "Humble Servant of God."

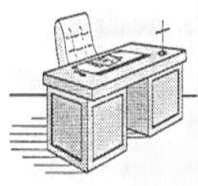

Pastor Jones
Doctor of Divinity
Clinical Psychologist
MBA in administration
Wilkins Preaching
Award
Humble servant of God

In Colossians 3, Paul encouraged the believers to put aside the deeds of the flesh including greed and selfishness because he says that they are idolatry. I think of the plague of media preachers who take advantage of their viewers and preach a prosperity gospel. Part of their appeal is to promise blessing if people send them their donations.

"A fantastic evangelist was on TV, and I sent him everything!"

Yes God will bless as we give, but we better be sure that we are giving to the right people who do not use our money for their financial benefit and to support their materialistic life style.

Paul was an example of one who looked to God and not man. He referred to himself as a slave of Jesus Christ. He learned that he could not trust the arm of the flesh. At the end of his life, he described his last thoughts in 2 Timothy 4. He encouraged Timothy to follow his example and hold to the Word of God. He shared that he had given his life for the sake of the gospel. He was also very vulnerable and shared his disappointment with people. Some like Alexander did him harm. Some like Demas deserted his team. Luke was with him for which he was thankful. However, at one point of his life all abandoned him. But he stated that, "However, the Lord stood with me and gave me strength to preach the Gospel"

The Christian Church and Idolatry

The Christian Church has battled idolatry over the years. There have always been problems and compromise as the church has come into relationship with the State. In 330 A.D. Constantine declared Christianity to be the state religion. Then, because there was no real conversion on the part of the people, they kept their paganism and added Christianity. Constantine adopt-

Mother and child cult

ed the mother/child cult which began during the time of the tower of Babel in Genesis. 11. Here we were introduced to Nimrod who according to historians married Semeramis, and had a baby named Tammuz. People began to worship Semeramis, who claimed to be a virgin, and her child. She is mentioned as the queen of heaven in Jeremiah 7:18, and she had become an object of worship. This cult passed on to other civilizations like the Greeks and the Romans. In Roman civilization the Romans worshipped Venus and her child Cupid.

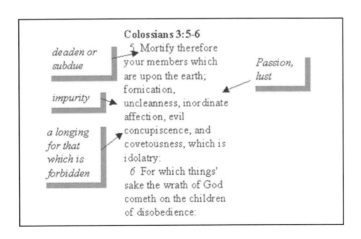

Colossians 3:5-6

deaden or subdue → 5 Mortify therefore your members which are upon the earth;

Passion, lust

fornication,

impurity → uncleanness, inordinate affection, evil

a longing for that which is forbidden → concupiscence, and covetousness, which is idolatry:
6 For which things' sake the wrath of God cometh on the children of disobedience:

CHAPTER 5

THE POWER AND PRACTICE OF THE WORD

In 2 Kings 18:5-8 we read that Hezekiah trusted in Lord and obeyed his Word. He put into practice the commandments of the Lord. The Lord prospered him as a result of this. This is the sowing and reaping principle. When we obey we are blessed, when we do not obey there will be discipline. We say that we are free to choose to obey or not, but we are not free to escape the consequences of our choices.

Now let's look at the purity, perpetuity, power, and practicality

God's refining work

of the Word. We read in Psalm 12:6 that the words of the Lord are pure as silver when it is refined. Similarly in Proverbs 30:5, we read that "every word of God is pure and is a shield to those who take refuge in Him." Purity reflects the holy nature of the Lord. We may use the medical word "uncontaminated" to describe the Word of the Lord.

While in college I came into contact with a popcorn salesman who had a unique style of selling his goods. At every basketball game he was in my section going up and down the steps, proclaiming, "Popcorn - dietetic, uncyclimated, tasty, and fresh." His sales pitch made you want to get out your cash and buy some. The word uncyclimated was a common one in those days which meant pure and without additives. The Word of the Lord is like that. It is pure and straight from the Lord.

"Dietetic, uncycli-mated, tasty, and fresh!"

The Word is also eternal. Isaiah 40:8 says that, "the grass
 withers, the flowers fade, but the Word of the
Lord endures forever". Psalm 119:89,152
declares: "Lord, your Word is forever. It is firm-
ly fixed in heaven". Jesus pronounces in
Matthew 24:35, "Heaven and earth will pass
away but my Words will never pass away".

The Word of God is powerful. Paul states in Romans 1:16: "I am
not ashamed of the gospel of Christ, because it is the power of
God for salvation; for the Jew first and then for the Gentile."
It is powerful enough to save the most wretched sinner.
Thank God for His grace. In Jeremiah 23:29, the Word is called a
hammer. A hammer smashes and destroys but is also used to
hit a nail which keeps wood
together.
The Word reveals our sin and
convicts us so that we may repent and put it away.
It destroys the works of the devil.
It also puts the pieces of our
shattered lives together.

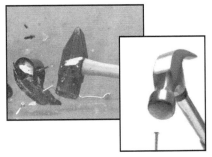

The prophet Jeremiah also shares that the Word is like fire.
It cleanses us from sin. It purifies us and refines us. I think we
need to catch the fire of God. I remember being in a Lutheran
church in Vienna. It was a grandiose church. There was no
central heating; instead each seat was warmed from beneath.
Some people probably thought the seat was too warm and it
made them uncomfortable. The Word of God will make us
uncomfortable as it reveals our sin. It will also give us a holy
inflamed passion that will truly motivate us to do things for the
glory of God.

In Hebrews 4:12 we read that:" The Word of the Lord is living and active and sharper than any two edged sword, and able to discern the thoughts and intentions of the heart."
A sword divides and will distinguish between what is real and what is false. It will also convict of sin.

In Ephesians 6, the Apostle Paul encouraged believers to put on the armor of God. He says we are to take the sword of the Spirit which is the Word of God. This was not a large sword that could be cumbersome. It was a smaller sword that could be swung easily to do as much damage as possible. We use the Word to  penetrate the hearts of people. Of course we do it in the power of God and energized by the Spirit.

Practicality of the Word
The Word of the Lord is inspired of God and profitable for teaching, reproof, correction and training in righteousness (2 Timothy 3:16). It is very practical. We know God's will and principles through His Word. The Word is to be known, understood, obeyed, and proclaimed.

It is not just for our knowledge. The Bible tells us that knowledge puffs up but love edifies. Jesus said that if we love Him we must obey His commands. (John 14 and 15).
Part of that obedience is to proclaim His Word. In fact after Paul shared with Timothy about the inspiration of the Spirit in 2 Tim. 3:16 and its practicality, he then exhorted Timothy to preach the Word in season and out of season.

Principles on the Word from the Old Testament

In the Old Testament we read of God giving the law to His people, the nation of Israel, after their deliverance from Egypt. In Deuteronomy 5, Moses reviews the Ten Commandments. He exhorted them to be careful to do all that the Lord had commanded. In Deuteronomy 6, he shared that these commandments were to be with the people as they crossed over to possess the land. He commanded this to sons and grandsons for all of their days. There was a promise that as they heard the Word and observed it, their days would be prolonged. They were also promised a good life and the prospect of multiplication as they entered the land flowing with milk and honey.

שְׁמַע יִשְׂרָאֵל: יהוה אֱלֹהֵינוּ, יהוה אֶחָד!

Sh'ma Yis-ra-eil: Adonai Eh-lo-hei-nu, Adonai Eh-chad!

Hear, O Israel: the Eternal One is our God,
the Eternal God alone!

בָּרוּךְ שֵׁם כְּבוֹד מַלְכוּתוֹ לְעוֹלָם וָעֶד!

Ba-ruch shem k'vod mal-chu-to l'o-lam va–ed!

Blessed is God's glorious majesty for ever and ever!

Moses then gave the famous *Shema* or "Hear O Israel, the Lord is one and you shall love the Lord your God with all your heart, soul and strength." These words should be on their hearts. They should also teach them diligently to their children and talk of them when they sat or walked, lay down or rose up. They were to put then as a sign on their hands and as frontlets between their eyes. They were to write them on their doorposts and gates.

Old wooden Mezuzah

34

As Israel was about to enter the Land, the Lord spoke to Joshua saying, "This book of the Law shall not depart from your mouth, but you shall meditate on it day and night, so that you may be careful to do all that is written in it, then you will be prosperous and then you will have success. (Joshua 1:8).

Psalm 1 speaks of the way of the righteous and the end of the ungodly. It begins stating that the man who is blessed is one who does not seek counsel from the ungodly or involve himself with sinners or sit with scorners. Instead, he delights in the law of the Lord. He thinks about this Law, and meditates on it day and night. We cannot read the Bible all day long, but we can constantly be thinking about it. Even in our sleep, after we have read or thought about the scripture, in some way the Word continues to minister to our hearts. There is promise of prosperity and fruitfulness to those who meditate on God's Word (Psalm 1: 3).

The Testimony of Creation and the Word - Psalm 19
Psalm 19 is short but very profound and instructive. I do not claim to be the world's expert on this Psalm, but it was the subject of my master's thesis at seminary. It was actually recommended to me by my Old Testament professor who felt more study needed to be made on this rich psalm. The psalm deals with God's revelation. First we have his general revelation found in His creation. Secondly we see his specific revelation in the Word of God.

The heavens declare the glory of God; and the firmament shows His handiwork. Psalms 19:1

The Psalm begins with the declaration that the heavens proclaim the glory of God. The sky speaks as it regularly changes from darkness to light. It shows the divine intelligence of the Creator. The sun also testifies of the creative hand of God as it rises and descends on a regular basis. The whole world benefits from its light and heat.

In Romans 1, Paul says that God reveals Himself to man through his creation and that man is without excuse in his rejection of God.

God also speaks through His Word. This is called His specific revelation. We read that the Word of the Lord is perfect. It comes from a holy and perfect God who does not lie. He makes no mistakes and His Word reflects that. The Word will revive souls. The statutes of the Lord are trustworthy. You can believe every Word. They will make even a simple person wise. The precepts of the Lord are right and give joy to our hearts. They are radiant and give light to our eyes. His Word is a lamp to our feet and a light to our eyes.

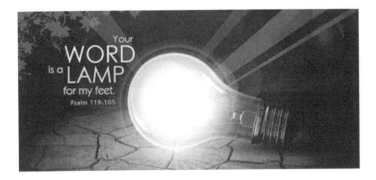
Your WORD is a LAMP for my feet. Psalm 119:105

The fear of the Lord that we see in His word is pure and endures.   When we go to the pharmacist, we want to be assured that the doctor will give us the right medicine with pure ingredients and no additives. That's how God's Word is. It is pure and sure. The Word is more precious than gold or silver.

In the old days California was known for its gold. There was a gold rush to get the gold. Explorers left all and went west to get the gold in "dem dar hills "as the expression goes. The reading and study-ing of the Word is worth eve-ry effort on our part. It is as though we were digging for gold. It is profitable to us to study His Word.

The Word is also sweeter than honey. It is desirable. It feeds our hungry souls. Then, we are warned by the Word. In keeping the Word there is reward. The word reward in the Hebrew means "heel". Everywhere we walk our heels go with us. So, when we keep God's Word His reward will go with us. Every step we take in obeying God will have its consequences. We reap rewards when we keep God's Word.

The Psalmist concludes with a prayer to the Lord that God would forgive him for his hidden faults. He asks for help in overcoming the power of sin. He then asks that his words and his heart attitudes would be pleasing to the Lord.

א

אַשְׁרֵי תְמִימֵי־דָרֶךְ הַהֹלְכִים בְּתוֹרַת יְהוָה׃
YHWH TORAH

אַשְׁרֵי נֹצְרֵי עֵדֹתָיו בְּכָל־לֵב יִדְרְשׁוּהוּ׃
EDAH

אַף לֹא־פָעֲלוּ עַוְלָה בִּדְרָכָיו הָלָכוּ׃
DEREK

אַתָּה צִוִּיתָה פִקֻּדֶיךָ לִשְׁמֹר מְאֹד׃
PIQQUWD

אַחֲלַי יִכֹּנוּ דְרָכָי לִשְׁמֹר חֻקֶּיךָ׃
CHOQ

אָז לֹא־אֵבוֹשׁ בְּהַבִּיטִי אֶל־כָּל־מִצְוֺתֶיךָ׃
MITSVAH

אוֹדְךָ בְּיֹשֶׁר לֵבָב בְּלָמְדִי מִשְׁפְּטֵי צִדְקֶךָ׃
MISHPAT

אֶת־חֻקֶּיךָ אֶשְׁמֹר אַל־תַּעַזְבֵנִי עַד־מְאֹד׃
CHOQ

1 ALEPH
Blessed are those whose ways are blameless,
who walk according to Yahweh's law.
Blessed are those who keep his statutes,
who seek him with their whole heart.
Yes, they do nothing wrong.
They walk in his ways.
You have commanded your precepts,
that we should fully obey them.
Oh that my ways were steadfast
to obey your statutes!
Then I wouldn't be disappointed,
when I consider all of your commandments.
I will give thanks to you with uprightness of heart,
when I learn your righteous judgments.
I will observe your statutes.
Don't utterly forsake me.

PSALM 119

This psalm is an acrostic poem in which the stanzas begin with
the different letters of the Hebrew alphabet. It is a psalm that is
replete with the blessings that come from obeying the Word of
the Lord. The word helps the godly to live a pure life (9, 11).
The Psalmist implores the Lord to open his eyes to the wonderful insights in the law of God (18). The Word brings joy to the
heart. The Psalmist desires to follow the word with all his heart.
His desire is to speak the Word before kings and not to be put to
shame (46). He praises God that he was afflicted so he could
learn the Word (71). He affirms that the Word is eternal and
stands firm in heaven (89). The Word makes us wiser than our
enemies and gives us more insight that our teachers (98,99).
The Word is a lamp to the feet of the psalmist and a light for his
path (105). The Word is more precious than gold (127).
The Psalmist is sad when people do not obey the law (136).
The Word also preserves life. (159). The Word brings
persecution but the Lord uses the Word to encourage (161).

CHAPTER 6

WHAT JESUS TAUGHT ABOUT THE WORD

We now come to the life and teachings of our Lord Jesus Christ in relation to the Word. We know that He is the Word incarnate, God Himself. He is the man who was tempted as we are and needed the Word to overcome the Devil. In Matthew 4 we read of this temptation.

First, He was baptized by John the Baptist and declared to be Son of God. He was then led by the Spirit into the wilderness to be tempted by the Devil. The Devil began his attack by stating, "If you are the son of God make these stones into bread." Jesus responded by  quoting Isaiah 40, "Man shall not live by bread alone but by every word that proceeds from the mouth of God."

The accuser then presented his second challenge. "If you are the Son of God, throw yourself from the pinnacle of the temple, for God will protect you; He will command His angels to help you." If you check the passage you will find that Satan misquoted the Scripture. Christ responded, "It is also written: Do not put the Lord your God to the test." The devil then took him to a high mountain and showed him all the kingdoms of the world and their splendor. He offered all of this to Jesus if He would just bow down and worship him. Jesus responded and said, "Get away from me, Satan, for it is written, Worship the Lord your God and serve Him only." Then the devil left.

We need to immerse ourselves in the word, mediate on it, memorize it, and use it against the enemy of our souls.

The Parable of the Four Soils

Jesus often taught his disciples by using parables or stories. In Mark 4 He had just chosen His disciples for the purpose of being with Him and sending them out to preach (Mark 4:13-19). They needed to know what to expect as they preached the Word. In the parable of the sower and the four soils, the seed is the Word of God (Mark 4:1-20).

The soils represent the types of response they were to expect as they sowed the seed. The first is the seed that falls along the path. The birds come and eat it up. These are those who hear the Word and then Satan comes and takes away the Word that was sown. There is then the seed which falls on rocky places. The soil is shallow. The seed springs up quickly because the soil is shallow, but when the sun comes out, the plants are scorched and they wither because they have no roots. This is the Word that is received with joy, but since these people have no roots in themselves, they last for only a short period. When trouble and persecution come, they quickly fall away.

Next, there is the seed that falls among the thorns. This seed grows up but is choked and does not bear fruit. This refers to people who hear the Word, but the worries of the world, the deceitfulness of wealth, the desires for other things, come in and choke the Word, making it unfruitful.

Finally, we have the seed which falls on good soil. It comes up, grows and produces a crop, multiplying thirty, sixty and even a hundred fold. These are those hear the Word, accept it and produce a great spiritual harvest.

This parable should encourage us all to be steadfast and persevering in preaching the Word of God. Our work for the Lord will not be in vain. (I Corinthians 15:58).

The Upper Room Discourse (John 13-16)

This passage tells about the final days of Jesus' earthly life. He had prepared His disciples, taught them, and sent them out. Now that His time to depart drew near He wanted to pass on what they needed to know as they continued His work.

After His anointing in Bethany, Jesus entered Jerusalem in triumphant glory and was hailed as the King of Israel. He spoke then of His upcoming death. He spoke of His witness to the people and His acceptance and His rejection.

It was right before the Passover Feast and He was with His disciples in the upper room for the evening meal.

Even Judas Iscariot, who had been prompted by the Devil to betray the Lord, was present. He began by washing the disciples' feet to leave them an example of serving one another. Then Jesus predicted His betrayal. After dismissing Judas to accomplish his devilish scheme Jesus shared His new commandment to love each other with the other disciples. This would be their mark of being true disciples. He then predicted Peter's denial.

After this, Jesus began to instruct the disciples about his departure and encourage them to carry on the work. He spoke of their ultimate destiny. He said He was going to prepare a place for them in the Father's house and He would come back for them to take them to be with Him there.
He stated that He is the Way, the Truth and the Life and that no one can come to the Father but by Him. He, Himself, is the truth and everything we read in the Word is truth. It all comes from Him. He then promised to do great things through them.

"We must dream great dreams...
And pray great prayers!"
Luis Palau

I remember hearing Luis Palau, the South American evangelist, speaking on this. Referring to John 14:12-15, he said that we must dream great dreams. Jesus promised," I tell you the truth, anyone who has faith in me, will do what I have been doing. He will do even greater things than these because I am going to the Father." Palau also preached that Jesus wants us to "Pray great prayers." The Lord stated in John 14:13, 14, "And I will do whatever you ask in my name, so that the Son may bring glory to the Father. You may ask me anything in my name and I will do it." Finally Palau suggested that we must, "do great things." The Lord concludes, "If you love me you will obey me".

> *We are left on earth to do the will of the Father.*
> *The Word must be known and obeyed.*

On another occasion in John 15, the Lord said that He is the vine

and we are the branches. We are told that, "If you abide in me and my Words abide in you, ask whatever you wish and it shall be done for you." John 15:7. Here we see the relationship between prayer and the Word. If we abide in or obey the Word, then God promises to answer our prayers.

In John 16, Jesus continued to speak of the Holy Spirit, saying that when Jesus left the Holy Spirit would be sent to be our comforter. He would be our teacher and guide. The Holy Spirit has come to give witness to Christ. He has come to convict the world of sin, righteousness, and the judgement to come.
The Holy Spirit uses the Word to reveal our sin. It reveals the holy nature of God and shows His standards in the Ten Commandments and the Sermon on the Mount. We see that our hearts are desperately wicked. We all have sinned and fall short of the glory of God. When we realize this, our hearts are burdened and we cry out to God for mercy.
The Word reveals the righteousness of God in Christ Jesus.
He has paid the penalty for our sin.
2 Corinthians 5:17 states that He has become our righteousness.
The Holy Spirit also uses the Word to reveal God's judgment upon sin. It is a warning to all to repent of our sins and turn to the Lord.

At the end of the Upper Room Discourse, the Lord prayed to His heavenly Father. He glorified the Lord (John 17). He said that He had done the will of God, and He asked the Lord to protect the disciples. He begged the Lord to sanctify the disciples in the truth which is His Word. We can be encouraged knowing that Jesus Christ is praying that for us right now. We are set apart and being conformed to the image of Christ through the Word. This is sanctification.

The Sermon on the Mount
The Sermon on the Mount found in Matthew 5-7 and in Luke is often referred to as the *"Magna Carta* of the Christian Life". Here we have the essential principles for true Kingdom Living. When we speak of the Kingdom of God, we must think of two realms. First, there is the future realm when Christ will return and set up His kingdom here on earth. We look forward to that. Then, there is the present Kingdom which is the reign of Christ in our hearts now through the Holy Spirit.

Be these.
Matthew 5:13-16

The Beatitudes teach us about Kingdom attitudes. We are called to be the light of the world and the salt of the earth. Christ declared Himself to be the fulfillment of the Law saying that He did not come to abolish the law but to fulfill it. All of His Word will be accomplished.

In this sermon the Lord admonishes His disciples not to be hypocritical like the Pharisees who were the big showmen, constantly seeking to display their external righteousness. Our giving and our prayers should not be on display for our self-glorification.

In Matthew 6, the Lord teaches us not to worry. God will give us all that we need when we seek first His Kingdom and His righteousness (Matthew 6:33).

In Matthew 7 the Lord speaks about the broad way and the narrow way. The broad way of religion leads to destruction and the narrow way of true faith leads to eternal life. He warns of false teachers and says that we will know them by their fruits. We can use the Word of God to test them. It is not those who say, "Lord, I did many great things for you, "who will enter the Kingdom. Miracles and even the casting out of demons are not the criteria. Christ will say to those people, "I never knew you." Only He who does the will of the Father will inherit the Kingdom.

False teachers and prophets have always been on the scene. Satan does everything He can to distort the truth. The nation of Israel which received the commandments and knew what was true, still fell into idolatry. They believed the false prophets and teachers of the pagan nations that surrounded them.

In Jeremiah 7, the prophet proclaims to the nation that they should hear the Word of the Lord and reform their ways and their actions. He tells them to not trust in deceptive words.

Changing their ways meant not oppressing the alien, the father-less or the widow. They were not to shed innocent blood. They should not follow other gods and trust in deceptive words.

The people of Israel were doing just that. They were building fires and offering sacrifices to the "queen of heaven" and worshipping other gods. They became stiff necked and did not obey the Lord. Jeremiah is told that they will not listen to him. The Lord states very clearly that, "Truth has perished, it has vanished from their lips." Jeremiah 7:28.

There is further rebuke and insight in Jeremiah 23. The prophet is broken because the land is full of adulterers. It is those prophets who follow an evil road and who use their power unjustly. There is even wickedness in the temple where the priests minister. God will bring judgment on them. The Lord tells the people to not listen to the prophets who speak about visions from their own minds. They were preaching peace and a sure hope, when God had promised judgment. These proph-ets had not been sent by God. True prophets stand in the council of the Lord and proclaim His words to His people.

The Lord rebukes them and says they dream false dreams and worship Baal. But, the Lord commends those who take the Word and preach it faithfully.

False Prophets
Lie About Their
Dreams
Jeremiah 23:25

He speaks against those who say something is an oracle from God when it is not. God will cast those people from His presence.

It troubles me when people I know say that God has spoken to them. Yes, God can guide us through His Word. However, these people state adamantly that they have had a Word from God. They claim to have the gift of prophecy. However, we know that God has already spoken through the prophets in the Bible and through His son, Jesus Christ (Hebrews 1:1-8).

People can certainly be deceived. There are people living here in Jerusalem who have what it called "the Jerusalem syndrome." They come here to prepare for the coming of the Lord because God has, "told them" to come. Some claim to have the gift of prophecy. One person thought he was a descendant of King Solomon and believed he was royal. He ended up in jail and was deported back to Egypt.

A few years ago during our ministry in Italy God taught us a great lesson about being careful with the people who claim to be believers. Not everyone who professes Christ is a true believer. Sometimes we get so excited about people "receiving the Lord," that we rush to call them believers and push them to the forefront.
This happened in Italy with a fellow whom I'll call Tony. He was a young man who heard the Gospel and made a "profession." Some of us were so excited about this that we decided to bring him to America with us to give his testimony. Let us remember that this was a new "convert". We are told in 1 Timothy 3 not to let a new convert assume leadership in the church.

Well, as this young man gave his testimony in several churches he became so happy about the responses of the people. They praised God for his conversion. Of course this went to his head. He came back to Italy and thought he was "anointed." He then began to think he was Christ Himself. Unfortunately, he had to be admitted to a mental hospital and his parents wanted to sue the church.

This experience taught me that we had better be careful how we push new believers. We are so anxious for visible fruit that we make mistakes. We need to be discerning and skeptical spiritually. We need to know what the Word says and be much in prayer in order to avoid mistakes like this.

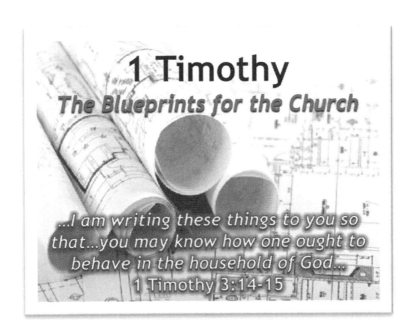

1 Timothy
The Blueprints for the Church
...I am writing these things to you so that...you may know how one ought to behave in the household of God...
1 Timothy 3:14-15

CHAPTER 7

AUTHENTIC OR FALSE?

The Tests of 1 John

In medieval European Cities, the cathedral became the center of the city. The rest of the city and the main thoroughfares circled around the cathedral. In the city of Vienna the center is dominated by St. Stephan's Cathedral, a massive gothic structure. On the left side of the entrance, right on the buildings, there are two curious looking items or symbols. One is a rod which is approximately one and half a yards long. The other is the figure of a bread roll imbedded into the building. These were the standards for the city. If you bought a length of cloth, you could take it to the cathedral and find out if you had been given the correct length. If the merchant had cheated you, he would be dunked in the Danube River. In the same way, if you bought a roll, you could take it to the cathedral and compare it to the roll etched there. If it did not conform to the size of the engraving near the door, than you could tell the police and the merchant would be arrested.

Standards are important.

Official Viennese linen ell and drapery ell length standards embedded in the cathedral wall

Jonathan Edwards

Jonathan Edwards was used of God in the First Great Awakening. Many people professed faith and there were many tears and much repentance. As a good pastor he wanted to make sure that those who professed Christ would demonstrate a genuine faith. He wrote a commentary on 1 John 4 in which he presented the Biblical tests for authentic faith in Jesus. John first encourages the believers to not believe every spirit but to test them whether they are from God. Many false prophets have gone into the world. How can we recognize these people? The first test is, does this person acknowledge that Jesus Christ has come in the flesh? If not, then he is not from God. He then states that whoever listens to them, (the apostles), knows God. This can mean today that it is those who listen to the Word of God who truly know God.

The next test is love. Whoever does not love does not know God. If we say we love God we must obey His commandments. If we have a desire to obey and follow the Lord, this is a good indication that we truly know the Lord. We also have the test of the spirit. Do we have the witness of the Spirit in our souls (see Romans 8).

1 John also suggest that these false prophets were with the Apostles but did not remain and so proved their false profession. John says that Christ's true disciples will continue in their faith. Of course, believers may fall and stumble. However, they will not continue in their sin.

The Christian life is a marathon race. We are all in the race. Being in a marathon we can fall and still get up and finish the race. If it were a sprint, most of us would lose the race.
Later on in 2 John, the apostle speaks of the joy of seeing his children walking in the truth. True love, he states, is following the Lord in obedience.
He states that many deceivers have gone into the world and tells us to watch out for those who do not continue in the teach-

Welcoming Jehovah Witnesses

ing of Christ. He says that we should not even invite these people into our homes. Probably we would think of those who invite the Jehovah Witness teams into their homes to debate their divergent views. I think this time of debate is fruitless. Just preach the Gospel to them and God will use it.

The Word can help us discern error and the truth will win out. Satan is a great deceiver. God, through the Word, can overcome deceit with truth.

"A LIE can travel halfway around the world while the TRUTH is still putting on its shoes." Mark Twain

Years ago in southern Italy, a Jehovah's Witness received a Gospel tract. He read it, studied it and turned to his Bible. He saw the truth and came to the Lord. He went back to his "kingdom hall" and shared the truth. Others came to the Lord and now that "kingdom hall" is an evangelical church. This is the triumph of the truth in the Word. I am reminded of another amazing story. The Jehovah's Witnesses are quite numerous in Europe. In fact in Italy there are more Jehovah's Witnesses than Protestants of all denominations.

In France one year, the Jehovah's Witnesses organized a conference in a big stadium. Members of an Operation Mobilization team went to distribute Gospel tracts to the participants. Soon the stadium filled up with people who had just received the tract. As soon as the chairman found out what had happened, he announced this to the people and told them to rip the tracts up and not read them. At that moment, 25, 000 people began to read with interest this evangelical Gospel tract. The truth of God will go out even in the midst of deceit and error.

WORD + SPIRIT = TRUTH

God's truth in a world of deception

CHAPTER 8

THE WORD GOES FORTH

The book of Acts has been referred to as the continuing work of Christ through His Apostles, in the spreading of the Kingdom of God. Jesus gave the outline in Acts 1:8.
He said, "But you shall receive power when the Holy Spirit has come upon you and you shall be my witnesses in Jerusalem, Judea and Samaria, and to the uttermost parts of the earth."
In Acts 1-7, we see the Word of God going forth in the city of Jerusalem.

The Gospel being preached in Jerusalem (Acts 1-7)

Chapter one begins with Jesus giving His disciples the promise of the coming of the Holy Spirit who would empower them to be His witnesses.   He then ascends to His Father and the disciples pray for ten days. In chapter 2 the Holy Spirit descends upon the believers, and miracles occur. Peter is then given the opportunity to preach the Gospel. Three thousand people repent, believe and are baptized. The church then devotes itself to the Apostles' teaching, prayer, fellowship and the Lord's Supper.

In Chapter 3, the apostles continue to perform miracles and preach the Gospel. They speak of the promise of Jesus coming again. In chapter 4, the opposition begins. It is mostly opposition from the religious leaders, but God miraculously delivers them and the preaching continues. Five thousand people come to the Lord. The disciples then get called up by the Magistrates. Jesus had said to them that they would be called before Magistrates and that the Holy Spirit would give them the words. We have seen God can do the same thing today.

A few years ago while serving in the city of Vienna, we saw many Iranians come to the Lord and be baptized. Many of them sought to become legitimate refugees. They knew that if they returned to Iran they would be subject to death. I was called up by several Austrian magistrates to testify on behalf of these Iranians as to the veracity of their professions of faith. It was an amazing experience. The magistrates asked me about them and what our faith was all about. I was able to articulate the Gospel to them. If fact one judge wanted to meet me for coffee and talk a little more about this and about American pop singers like Bruce Springsteen.

On another occasion, I was called up by a man I will call George, a Catholic theologian who was in charge of the cult department (formerly called the Inquisition Committee). He had been contacted by the police to investigate these Iranians who were being baptized. He called me in for questioning. I decided to take my friend, Amadeus, with me. He was Polish and a former Catholic seminarian, who spoke good German and could help me understand better. As we walked into the theologian's office I was

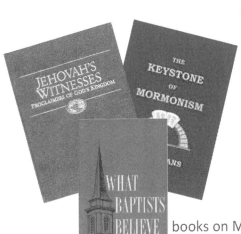

shocked. Amadeus greeted him warmly.
It turned out that he and the theologian had been in seminary together.
What a divine coincidence. George then began to ask me about the Baptists. I noticed that in his office he had a library with a section on cults. It included books on Mormons, Jehovah witness, and Baptists.

I explained the Biblical doctrine of Baptists and that we wanted to be faithful to the Word of God. I went through some of the stories in the book of Acts. He was enthralled.

At the end, he said, "I will have to visit your church someday." What a great opportunity.

In Acts 4:13 we read of the religious leaders who marveled at the boldness and authority of Peter and John. They knew that Peter and John were uneducated fisherman, and the only explanation for their boldness was the fact that they had been with Jesus. They spoke with divine unction and power. They knew whom they had believed. It is amazing how transforming it can be when you meet the right person.

When I was in high school I had a very low image of myself. I suffered with acne, I was a little overweight and had other problems. An English teacher gave us the assignment to write our philosophy of life.

My paper was very negative as you can imagine.

The teacher called me in and said, "Albert, you have a problem with your image. You need a girlfriend."

So, my assignment was to find a girlfriend. I found one and my life was changed.

I felt accepted and loved. My image changed. I was a new man. After a two year relationship, however, my girlfriend left me and I became depressed and downcast again.

God used this experience, however, as I began to seek someone who would love me unconditionally and forever. I didn't realize it, but I was seeking God, the only one who loves us like that.

When I heard that Billy Graham was in town, I went to hear him and when he gave the altar call I went forward and committed my life to Christ. The counselor who spoke with me after the meeting shared John 3:16 which says, "God so loved the world that He gave his only begotten son that whoever believes in him should not perish but have eternal life." When I began to experience God's perfect and unconditional love and acceptance my whole outlook changed.

Praying for Power
Acts 4:23-41 tells about Peter and John being warned not to speak or teach anymore in the name of Jesus and being threatened by the authorities. Then comes the account of the believers gathering for an earth shaking prayer meeting. They prayed a prayer based on Psalm 2 where the Psalmist speaks of those rulers who conspired against the son of God. Since they represented the Son of God they also were the victims of the attacks of the religious establishment. They prayed for boldness.
The believers prayed, the place shook and they began to preach the Word of God courageously.

Probably the greatest lessons I have learned about prayer have come from Korean believers. I read the book on prayer by Paul Yonggi Cho, the pastor of the largest church in the world in Seoul, Korea. The Koreans are known to be people who spend hours in prayer.

Prayer Mountain Retreat in South Korea

They even have a prayer mountain where they go to give themselves to prayer. When my wife and I had problems conceiving children, I wrote to the church in Korea asking them to pray for us. God blessed us with 3 beautiful daughters.

During our service in Italy, I got to know a Korean church which was comprised of many opera singers. I heard they had a wonderful choir, and since we were going to have a mission's conference, I decided to invite their choir to be part of it. When they arrived, they immediately asked me if they could go to the back room and pray. "Great!" I said. The twenty-five member choir followed me into the back room. I then discovered prayer, Korean style. They all began to pray together at the same time, of course, in their own language. I tell you, the place shook. I have never experienced such a meeting. During the meeting they sang a heavenly song sung in beautiful Italian. As the meeting went on I said to all that we should pray for Korea. As I started to pray, they started to pray Korean style. The place shook again.

The Italians who were present never experienced anything like this and were awestruck. At the end of the meeting, I invited the

Korean-style praying

Korean choir to come out for ice cream. They immediately said, "Pastor, we must pray first." We went to the back room again and started to pray Korean style. I learned a great lesson.

Milan Cathedral - Italy

A few weeks after that, the Koreans invited me to preach at an open air meeting near the Duomo (cathedral) of Milan.
We gathered in the busy square. They began to pray in power, they sang majestically, and then I preached. I felt totally under the control of the Spirit. He gave me words and unction that I had never before experienced.

In the last few verses of Acts 4 we read that the believers were of one heart and soul and that they became a sharing community. They communicated their message with power and grace. Each one contributed to the common need. The chapter ends with the mention of Barnabas, a true example of generosity, an open heart, and an obedient spirit.

Ananias and Sapphira

In Acts 5:1-11, the Lord purifies His church. The church was united in Spirit, but even one sin in the body can spoil everything.
Here is the story of a couple who demonstrated a spirit that was contrary to Barnabas' spirit of generosity. They sold a piece of property and brought some of the money to the apostles implying that it was the whole amount of the sale. They lied to the Holy Spirit. God put Ananias and Sapphira to death because of their sin. God is serious about sin in the body.

The Apostles continued to preach the Gospel after the purging. God uses clean vessels. They performed many signs and wonders which confirmed the word they were preaching. Of course, what they did drew the jealously of the religious establishment. The people were astonished at the signs they observed. Many were added to the church (Acts 5:12-16).

In Acts 5:17-32, we see the apostles persecuted by the religious establishment because of jealousy. They arrested the apostles and put them in jail. The angels went to work and one of them opened the door of the jail and brought them out, telling them to, "Go, stand in the temple courts, and tell the people the full message of this new life."

They began to preach and of course this perplexed the Sanhedrin. They did not want to hurt the apostles for fear the people would stone them. In the plan of God they were brought before the Sanhedrin to testify. Their accusation was pointed and direct. "We gave you  strict orders not to teach in his name, but you have filled Jerusalem with your teaching and are determined to make us guilty of this man's blood." Peter and the others responded "We must obey God and not man," and they began to preach the Gospel about Jesus who died, was resurrected and who gives repentance and forgiveness of sins to Israel.

After the preaching of the Gospel, the religious leaders were furious with the Apostles. They wanted to kill them. However, God intervened and used a venerated teacher of the law, a Pharisee who was greatly honored by the people. He stood up in the Sanhedrin and began to reason with the leaders. He talked about others who had led rebellions but were quickly defeated. He advised the religious leaders to leave the Apostles alone. He knew that if what they were doing was of human origin, they would fail. If it was of God, then nothing could stop it. They would be fighting against God. When we are attacked, let us have confidence that God can intervene on our behalf and even use men who are not completely sympathetic to our faith.

Gamaliel persuaded the leaders to let the disciples go but they flogged them and told them not to preach. This did not stop the apostles. They rejoiced that they had been counted worthy of suffering disgrace for the name of Jesus. Day after day in the temple and from house to house, they continued to teach and proclaim the good news of Jesus Christ. When we preach Jesus we should expect opposition. It is often a sign that we are doing the right thing. We should continue to preach and teach about Jesus. Persistence pays off.

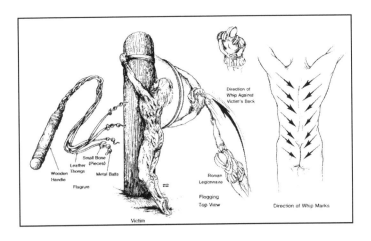

In any sport, the goal is winning. We must keep our goals in mind and persevere in the pursuit of our goals. The key is practice, practice, practice. As a young man Magic Johnson always kept a basketball with him. He dribbled it to school. He took it to bed with him. He shot, shot, and shot to develop his accuracy.

Magic Johnson and Larry Bird

The same was true for Pete Maravich, Larry Bird, and others. They ate, slept and drank basketball.

Growing up I was always interested in sports. I thought it was a manly thing to do and also the girls liked athletic guys.

I wrestled, played baseball and football, and even threw the javelin. During my freshman year in high school, I managed to make the wrestling team. It is a tough sport which demands a lot of discipline and strength. Maintaining my weight and doing exercises was really hard.

On one occasion, during a team practice, I was pinned by one of my classmates. After the match, I saw what the coach had written about me in his play book. It said, "You quit!" That statement propelled me into action. I never wanted to be known as a quitter. I started an intensive weight lifting program. Every time I pumped those bars, I thought of my coaches' statement. It paid off. The next year in high school, I made the football team and played until I graduated. I never got hurt. I was commended as a linebacker and even captained the defensive junior varsity team. I remember in one practice, I was lined up to tackle a 300 pound monster.

I took my position and when the whistle blew, I attacked him and he landed flat on his back with a big thump. Nothing ever felt so good!

When I went to college, I was too small to try out for football at the University of Maryland. I did excel however, in my gym classes. When we did wrestling, the teacher heard that I had wrestled some in high school. I was to wrestle a number of other students until I lost. I kept pinning one after another and I think finished off the entire class. What sweet revenge.

When I took judo for a gym class, I was able to become the champion of the class. My wrestling past helped. You could say I was the judo champion at the University of Maryland because this gym class was the only one they offered. Perseverance pays off.

Here is a formula I learned a few years ago about obtaining our goals. We must first have clear cut goals. We must know what we are aiming at. When a lady attempted to swim from the shores of California to Catalina Island, she quit around 100 meters from the goal. A fog had set in and she could not see her goal even though it was only a short distance away. This discouraged her. If she had been able to see the shore of Catalina that was only a short distance away, this may have given her the extra impetus needed to reach her goal.

Florence Chadwick

Once we have a clear cut goal, we must pursue it with diligence. We must commit ourselves wholeheartedly. We must sometimes realign. We must then persist and persist until we obtain our goal. A young man with a stuttering problem fell in love with a girl. He worked on his speech and kept on repeating to himself, "Will you go out with me". He finally mustered up the courage to ask her out. She accepted and said, "You must have practiced that for a long time." She was impressed with his perseverance.

Our goal is the same as that of the apostles; we want to preach Christ until He returns. God can help us because He gives us the power and strength to keep on keeping on.

Priorities
In Chapter 6, we are presented with one of the first challenges to the unity of the early church. Praise God that the church was growing. Of course, wherever there are people there are problems and when believers are of different nationalities that in itself can be a tremendous cause of strife and misunderstanding. We see here a conflict between Grecians Jews and those of the Aramaic speaking Jewish community. The problem was with the daily distribution of food for the widows. The Aramaic community felt that their widows were being overlooked.

The Apostles then went into action. They called the disciples together and said it would not be right for them to neglect the ministry of the Word to wait on tables. They delegated the responsibility asking them to choose seven men who were full of the Spirit and wisdom.

They were to be given the responsibility of feeding the widows. This would free up the Apostles to give themselves to the Word and to prayer. They chose these men, prayed for them and then laid their hands on them.

Here we have the principle of priorities. Human and physical needs are important. However, spiritual needs take precedence. As we seek first the Kingdom of God and His righteousness, the Lord promises to meet our needs. The Lord's Prayer which could more appropriately be called the disciples prayer, begins with our appeal to God and worship of His name. We then pray for the Kingdom of God to come. We pray for souls to be reached and nations to be transformed by the power of God. Does this mean pastors and ministers do not do physical work? No.

Jesus helped. Jesus healed people. He had compassion. I think we must not only preach the Gospel but live the Gospel. We must lead by example. It has been my practice to not only preach and evangelize, but also to help where needed using my car to take people places, or helping people to move.

Lead by Example - Leadership is about ACTION, not POSITION.

Then comes a progress report in Acts 6:7 The Word of God spread. The number of disciples in Jerusalem increased rapidly and many priests became obedient to the faith. This was the sovereign work of God because only He can add to the church. However, it was also the result of the faithful preaching of the Gospel by the Apostles. They lived the message and proclaimed it faithfully.

The Word of God is being spread today by those who preach the Word, and also by those who distribute Bibles, tracts and literature. We can rejoice in the work of the Gideon's who not only leave Bibles in hotels but who also give out

A Gideon's Bible

Bibles. My friend, Gienek Trichionkowski, is a pastor in Rybnik, Poland. He is a multi-tasked pastor who cares for two churches, heads up the ministry of Evangelism Explosion in Poland, and coordinates the ministry of Joni and Friends, a ministry that supplies wheelchairs to the needy. However, one of his greatest joys is to distribute the Gideon Bible to the Polish Army.

The Word goes out, and people become disciples or true followers of Jesus. A disciple is a learner. The word in the Greek also means a martyr. There has been a big discussion about discipleship in the Christian world today. We know that Jesus poured his life into his 12 disciples. One of them betrayed him. The others went on to preach the Gospel and disciple others. The Gospel spread through the multiplication principle. However, discipleship begins with decisions. The Gospel must be preached and people must believe. They must decide to follow Jesus. I know that God is sovereign but from the human perspective people must believe in their hearts that Jesus is Lord and must commit themselves to follow him.

We also see that a large number of priests became obedient to the faith. This encourages me here in the city of Jerusalem where there are many religious people including Jews, Christians, and Muslims. They are fervent in their beliefs. God loves religious people but hates religious hypocrisy.

Jesus rebuked the religious Pharisees for their hypocrisy.
I find an interest among the religious to have a personal rela-
tionship with God. Jesus encountered a religious man named
Nicodemus. He was a Pharisee who came to Jesus during the
night. He spoke to Jesus and recognized that He was sent from
God. Jesus told him that he must be born again. He was saying,
unless you are born from above, you cannot see the Kingdom of
God. God must work in your life.

One time I was visiting a Catholic Seminary in Krakow, Poland
with my friend Amadeus, a former Roman Catholic seminarian

who had studied in
that seminary.
We got there at lunch
time and the chief
monsignor invited us
to eat with him.
I got to sit next to
him and spoke with
him in Italian since he
was from an Italian
order named the
Salesians of Don

Don Bosco

Bosco, a well-known Italian priest. We talked about the Lord and
the hope of the Christian faith. I tried to bring in my testimony.
It was a helpful conversation. When I left, a priest came over to
me.
He had been a classmate of Amadeus at the Seminary. He was
now a teacher of theology at the Seminary. He came up and
asked me "What does it mean to be born again?" Surprised at
his question I began to explain, rejoicing in this great opportunity.

One of the greatest experiences of my life was to be involved with evangelistic outreaches in Eastern European countries. One such outreach was in the city of Bratislava, Slovakia which is one hour east of Vienna. We were there with a team of internationals which included Americans, English, Slovakians, Polish and others. Korky Davey of Open Air Campaigners who has always had a vision for the city of Bratislava, was with us. Now that vision was being fulfilled and I was his right hand man.

Korky Davey

As we surveyed the place, we noticed a big volleyball tournament in the square where we would have our evangelistic con-

Čumil - "the Watcher"

cert the next day. I worried that the volleyball tournament would continue the next day. As we continued to survey the area, we stopped by a statue of a man peeking out from under a manhole cover. As we did this, somebody came along and pushed me aside. I was taken aback and looked to see who had pushed me. It was the body guard of the president of Slovakia who was making the way for the coming of the "King".

This provided a great illustration. As these men were preparing the way for the coming of the President, we were going to preach the Gospel in preparation for the coming of THE King.

The next evening we set up for our outdoor concert and evangelistic meeting. I was scheduled to preach. Normally, we just use a small Bible when preaching so we do not look too preachy.

My friend and fellow pastor in Austria, Rob Prokop introduced me and said I would be preaching from the Bible. Normally, we do not say this because we do not want to scare people away. But this time no one left. Then I began to preach the simple Gospel as I had learned it from Evangelism Explosion. I was amazed that when I gave the invitation around 100 people lined up including a few Roman Catholic priests.

Rob Prokop

Yes, there is a great hunger even among religious leaders for the simple message of the Gospel.

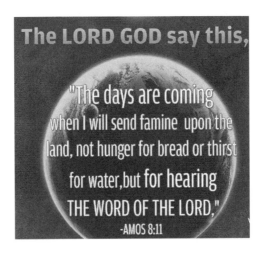

The LORD GOD say this, "The days are coming when I will send famine upon the land, not hunger for bread or thirst for water, but for hearing THE WORD OF THE LORD," -AMOS 8:11

CHAPTER 9

FRUITS OF PERSECUTION

In Acts 7 we read the powerful testimony of Stephen before the religious leaders. It was a bold assertion of the Gospel with a penetrating proclamation of the sin of the leaders in rejecting all the prophets that God had sent them throughout their history. They rejected Joseph who was betrayed by his brothers. They rebelled against Moses and turned to idolatry. In fact, Stephen said that there was never a prophet that their fathers did not persecute including the ones who predicted the coming of Jesus. And now, they themselves had betrayed and murdered Him. They had received the Law but had not obeyed it.

Of course, the religious leaders were enraged. As they vented their anger upon him, the Scripture says that he was filled with the Holy Spirit. He saw Jesus standing at the right hand of the Father. Could it be that if the Jews had accepted the message of Stephen, God would have forgiven them and Christ would come back again right then? Unfortunately, we will never know the answer because  they rejected the message and stoned him to death. His final words were similar to the words of Jesus, "Forgive them for they know not what they do."

In the spring of 2012, I preached a message at the Jerusalem

When your house is built on sand

Baptist church. It was from Matthew 7 on the need to build our lives on the solid rock using Jesus' illustration about a wise man who built his house on solid rock as opposed to the foolish man who built it on sand. When the winds and storm came, the house of the wise man stood because it had a firm foundation.

The next morning, I received a text message that somebody had attacked our church. I went down right away and discovered that some anti-Christian vandals had punctured the tires of several cars in the parking lot and had sprayed graffiti on the walls of the church saying, "death to Christians," and, "Jesus, the son of a whore." I was shocked but the Lord used it for good. Many of our neighbors came

Hebrew graffiti on our Church

to give support and some brought flowers. My Jewish friend and his Rabbi came and supported us. The Lord gave opportunities to give a testimony. I was also invited to appear on Israeli television to be interviewed about the situation. God helped me to explain. Even a representative from the Ministry of the Interior came to support us during this crisis.

The next day I went to Bethlehem with my friend and colleague, Terry Hill. Jerusalem Baptist Church was to receive a plaque to thank us for singing in Manger Square on Christmas Eve.

We got there and met the mayor and vice mayor and I told them about what had happened to our church. The vice mayor stated then that as Christians we must forgive. He said that during the intifada, his twelve year old daughter was killed and he was shot eight times. They were innocent victims caught in a cross fire. His last words to me were: "We must forgive. This is what Jesus did." I left in tears.

Church on the Move
In Acts 8-28 we see the church on the move. Chapter 8 is pivotal. The gospel has gone forth in Jerusalem. Stephen was martyred. Saul was there to witness his faithful testimony and encouraged the stoning. He guarded all of the clothing of the perpetrators.

We read of a great persecution that broke out against Christians in Jerusalem. This was good for the church. We notice that the persecution forced the church to scatter around Judea and Samaria. What happened as they were scattered?
They continued to preach the Gospel which led to a great revival in Samaria.
Philip was sent there to proclaim Christ. Great joy came upon the city. They had an interesting encounter with Simon the Sorcerer. It says that he believed

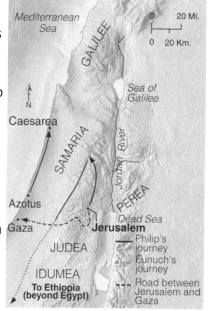

and was baptized. He saw the power of the apostles and asked if he could buy their power. They confronted him and told him that this could not be bought. They told him to repent of his sin.

Philip and the Ethiopian eunuch

In this section we also have the story of the amazing encounter between Philip and the Ethiopian eunuch on the road from Jerusalem to Gaza. I call this a divine triangle. God desired to save this Ethiopian eunuch. He put it on the heart of his messenger Philip to leave the great revival in Samaria and take the road to Gaza. There Philip met a man who was reading the book of Isaiah. This important person, the treasurer of the queen of Ethiopia, had been to Jerusalem to worship God. He just so happened to be reading from Isaiah 53 which speaks about a sheep going to slaughter and the lamb who does not open his mouth, referring to the Messiah who would first come as an innocent lamb to sacrifice Himself for the sins of the world. This divine encounter led to the conversion of this Ethiopian. Historians tell us that this Ethiopian led a revival in his land.

In Acts 13-28, we have the beginning of the spread of the Word around the world. We read of the first international church in the plan of God. It is the church at Antioch and it became the base for the Word of God to be preached to the ends of the earth. It was a model church, international and missionary. It sent out Paul and Barnabas with the message of the Gospel. That message went out to Asia, Macedonia, and onto Rome.

Today the Word continues to be preached
to the ends of the earth.

CHAPTER 10

GOD'S PROVISION

Purification of the Temple

King Hezekiah returned to the Lord. He was zealous for the purity of the people of God. In 2 Chronicles 29 we read of the King opening and repairing the doors of the Temple. The Temple was the center of worship for the nation of Israel.

The King appointed priests and Levites to minister in the temple. Their ministry was to lead in worship by song and sacrifice. They were ordered to make meat, blood, grain and other types of sacrifices to the Lord.

We celebrate Yom Kippur every year to remember the time when the high priest would sacrifice a lamb on the altar in the holy of holies in the temple. He would first lay his hands on the lamb symbolizing the transfer of the sins of the people to the Lamb.

Hezekiah also reinstituted the Passover celebration to remember the plight of the nation of Israel in Egypt. They were delivered as they sacrificed lambs and put the blood on their doorposts. The Angel of the Lord passed over their homes and they were not judged.

In the Bible, blood represents life. In Leviticus 17:11 blood becomes the basis for the forgiveness of sin. It is the way atonement is made for sins and trespasses. Atonement means a covering for sin. In Hebrews 9:22, we read, "In fact, the law requires that every-thing be cleansed with blood, and without the shedding of blood there is no forgiveness."

The Passover Lamb gives us a beautiful picture of God's provision for our sin in our Lord Jesus Christ. Christ was the Lamb of God who took away the sin of the world. He died for our sins once for all (Hebrews 9:26-28). Because of Christ's sacrifice we have peace with God (Romans 5:1). We have been reconciled to God (2 Corinthians 5). We have been brought to God (1 Peter 3:18). Christ died for sins once for all, the just for the unjust, in order to bring us to God (1 Peter 3:18). Through his blood our worship is acceptable before God. Psalm 26: 6,7 states, "I wash my hands in innocence and go around Your altar, Lord, raising my voice in thanksgiving and telling about Your wonderful works." Psalm 134:2 says, "Lift up your hands in the holy place, and praise the Lord. " In 1 Timothy 2:8 we read, "Therefore I want men in every place to pray, lifting up holy hands without anger or argument."

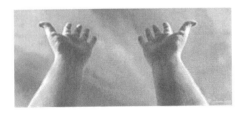

We can live the holy lives that God desires only because of the sacrificial death of Christ. We have died with Him and should no longer be controlled by our sin nature. However, as 1 John says, "If we say we are without sin, then we lie and the truth of God is not in us. However, if we sin we have an advocate with the Father who intercedes for us." But, he says that if we confess our sins God is faithful and righteous to forgive our sins and to cleanse us from all unrighteousness. (1 John 1:8, 9)

The sacrifice of God is also the basis for our unity in the faith. We have been brought together in unity by the blood of Jesus. In Ephesians 2:13-16 we read, "But now in Christ Jesus, you who were far away have been brought near by the blood of the Messiah. For He is our peace, who made both groups one and tore down the dividing wall of hostility. In His flesh, He did away with the law of the commandments in regulations, so that He might create in Himself one new man from the two, resulting in peace. He did this so that He might reconcile both to God in one body through the cross and put the hostility to death by it."

Recently I was at a Promise Keepers conference here in Jerusalem. Promise Keepers is a men's ministry dedicated to helping men live holy lives before God, their family, their church and their community. One of their goals is reconciliation. They wish to bring believers of different denominations and of different ethnic origins together in Christ. At one of their pastors conferences they had black, Hispanic, and white pastors, and Indians serve one another and pray for one another.

Practicing our Faith (Our offering to the Lord)

As Christ offered Himself as a sacrifice, so we offer ourselves as sacrifices. When we worship and praise the Lord, we are offering a sacrifice to the Lord. (Hebrews 13:13).
As priests of God (1 Peter 2) we are also to intercede for others. This was the ministry of the Aaronic priests and Levites.
The great High Priest would offer a sacrifice for the sins of the people and then spend time in intercession. Christ is praying for us (Hebrews). We, too, pray for others (1 Timothy 2:1-4)

Doing good and helping the needy are acts of worship before the Lord. (Hebrews 13:14, James 1:27). We must always help the poor (Psalm 41:1-3; Psalm 35:10, 70:5, 74:21).
The Proclaiming of the Gospel is one way we make an offering to the Lord (Romans 14:1-22). Isaiah 58 has always been an encouragement to me. The prophet shares what true fasting is all about. It is to help the weak, deliver people, feed the poor, clothe the naked, and help the oppressed. We will be blessed as we do this. Our light will shine. The glory of God will follow us, and God will direct us.

Recently I heard Tommy Barnett of the First Assembly of God Church in Phoenix, Arizona speak. I had heard about him during my church growth studies for my Doctor of Ministry. He was greatly influenced by Dr. Jack Hyles and especially by their bus ministry. Pastor Barnett spoke of God's love for the poor. He has started a "Dream Center" in Los Angeles where his son is the pastor and God has blessed. He said, "When you reach out to people that no one wants, God sends you people that everyone wants."

He reaches out to the poor and needy in Los Angeles and God sends them Hollywood people who attend the church.

The Point of our Preaching

God's provision for our sin in Christ becomes the main point of our preaching. In 1 Corinthians 15 the Apostle Paul says that the Gospel he received he passed on to them. It is that Christ died for our sin, was buried, and rose again. In 1 Corinthians 2 Paul states that when he came to the Corinthians he did not come with persuasive words of wisdom but in demonstration of the power of God. He desired to preach nothing but Jesus Christ and Him crucified. He who was a brilliant, theological preacher, focused his preaching on the simple but profound message of the Gospel.

A HEAVENLY COMMISSION CONFIRMED

"A few days before my father's death, he gathered his family around his bed to share his last wishes.

He told my mother how much she would be getting every month from his pension. He told her to stay in the house since it would be the best situation for her.

"You and your sister, take care of your mother," he told me. He then told us to get ten death certificates for his insurance policies (he was an insurance agent in his working days). He said to have the funeral at the Ippolito funeral home (friends of the family).

Finally, he looked me in the eye and said, "Albert, and you preach!" That was his last wish.

I knew what that meant. It meant to preach the Gospel at the funeral and continue to preach it to the world.

At the funeral, the Lord gave me the opportunity to preach to 300 of our friends and relatives.

I have continued to preach the Gospel of our Lord Jesus Christ. My heavenly Father commissioned me according to Matthew 28:18-20 and my earthly father confirmed it."

CHAPTER 11

PASSIONATE PREACHING

The Preaching of Sin, Repentance and Faith

The three parables in Luke 15 illustrate God's love for the lost in a powerful way. He is like the shepherd searching for the lost sheep. He is like the woman looking for the coin. And, He is like the father who embraces His prodigal son on his return home. The Apostle Paul tells us in Romans 15:14-22 that it is our priestly duty to proclaim the Gospel. When we lead  the Gentiles to Christ we are offering them as a sacrifice for the Lord.

King Hezekiah was a king with an evangelistic heart. He had a passion for God, a hatred for idolatry, an obedient heart, and a desire for His people to return to God. In II Chronicles 30:1-12, we read of him sending couriers around the country to tell them to return to God and to return to Jerusalem to celebrate the Passover. These couriers were ridiculed and mocked.

We should also expect rejection and scorning. If we are going to see revival we must be a people who seek to win the lost.

Principles of Effective Evangelism

1. What is this? A math formula? 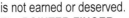 $$HP + CP + CC = MI$$

It is a formula I learned from Bill Hybels. The **MI** signifies **Maximum Impact**. That is the Goal. To have maximum impact for the Kingdom of God. How is this achieved? There are three means. **HP** means **High Potency**. We must first of all have a life that is potent and that reflects the life of Jesus. **CP** means **Close Proximity.** We must be in contact with non-Christians. Too often we hang out only with Christians. Jesus hung out with sinners and publicans. **CC** stands for **Clear Communication.** We must learn how to share the Gospel clearly and powerfully. I use the hand illustration to do this.

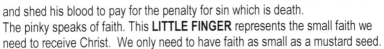

The **THUMB** points up to heaven and signifies that Heaven is a free gift which is not earned or deserved.
The **POINTER FINGER** points to a person with one finger and points to ourselves with three. This speaks of our sin.
We point one finger to another person and three towards ourselves. We are all sinners according to Romans 3:23.
The **MIDDLE FINGER** which is the largest, speaks of God who is a just God who must punish sin. He is also a God of love who does not want to punish us for sin but desires to show mercy. Where do justice and mercy meet? They meet in Jesus who is represented by the **RING FINGER**. The ring speaks of Christ as our bridegroom and we as his bride. He came to die on the cross and shed his blood to pay for the penalty for sin which is death.
The pinky speaks of faith. This **LITTLE FINGER** represents the small faith we need to receive Christ. We only need to have faith as small as a mustard seed.

2. **Sowing and Reaping:** Evangelism is sowing the Gospel. Some sow the seed of the gospel, some reap but God causes the increase. In Galatians 6 we read that what we sow we reap. Psalm 126 speaks of the famer who sows seeds with tears. He will come rejoicing bringing in the harvest. 2 Corinthians 9 says that those who sow bountifully will reap bountifully and those who sow sparingly will reap sparingly. This verse is speaking of giving but can also be applied to the principle for evangelism. We need to keep spreading the seed of the Word of God.

3. We have the **parable of the sower and the seed** in Matthew 13. As the sower sowed the seed, some of the seed fell on the path and the birds ate it up. Then some of the seed fell on rocky ground. It sprang up quickly but when the sun came up it withered because it had no roots. Some other seeds fell among thorns that choked it so that it bears no fruit. Finally, other seed falls on good ground and the plants grow and multiply.

4. **Overflow Principle**: In 1 Tim. 4:16, we find a complete description of a philosophy of ministry. This verse is my life verse. In the chapter, the Apostle writes to Timothy about how he can be useful and successful in his church. In

light of the false doctrine that was being propagated around Ephesus, Paul exhorts Timothy to nourish himself on the Word of God. He tells him to be an example and dedicate himself to the reading and preaching of the Word of God. The last verse of the chapter say, "Pay close attention to yourself and to your teaching, persevere in doing this. Then, as you do this you will save yourself and those who hear you. He is saying, Timothy, look to your own life first. Are you desiring to be like Christ? Are you examining your heart and cultivating it? Are you reading and studying the Word of God and making it a part of your life and ministry? Are you seeking to be accurate in your teaching? As Timothy does these things he will be used of God to save others. His life will overflow and influence others for the Kingdom of God.

5. **Examine the Soil**: The Parable of the sower and the seed encourages us in our outreach. We read about it in Mark 4 and Matthew 13. We have the sower who sows the seed along the path. The seed which falls on the path is quickly eaten by the birds. This represents Satan who comes to take the Word of God away from people.  The seed also falls on rocky ground, but since it has no roots it dies quickly. These seeds represent those who hear the Word but it does not penetrate their lives. Some seed then falls among thorns that choke it out and it produces no fruit. These represent people who hear the word but the cares of life and the desire to be rich choke out or kill the fruit. There is then the seed which is sown on good ground. The seed falls on the ground and grows abundantly yielding even thirty times what was sown.

6. **Divine flexibility**: In 1 Corinthians 9 Paul writes that when he communicates to Jews he becomes a Jew, and when he communicates to a Roman, he becomes a Roman. To the Greek a Greek. He sought to get to know the

language and mentality of the people he was speaking to. We must analyze our audience. This takes spending time with them. We do our best to not offend them. We let the gospel offend them. We speak their language.

7. **Praying for open doors:**
   According to Colossians 4, Paul asked prayer for open doors and a clear message. It is God who opens and shuts doors. I remember praying this prayer when I was in Poland. I always prayed to be an encouragement and to be able to preach in the open air. I had spoken in a youth gathering and in a church, but I really wanted to preach in the open air. On Sunday afternoon, our last day before we would head back to Vienna, God answered my prayer. We were doing a children's meeting in a building when we heard some music in the background. Amadeus, my Polish friend, and I went to see what was going on. It was the local Polish idol contest with 400 people in attendance. Amadeus went up to the organizer and pointed to me. He said that I was a popular singer named Al Cappuccino. I got this name on another occasion in Poland when I was about to sing and give testimony. The presenter introduced me as 'Al Cappuccino'. Amadeus asked the organizer if we could sing and the organizer said, "OK." "How long?" we asked. "Twenty minutes." In those twenty minutes we sang gospel songs like "Oh Happy Day", "Down by the Riverside" and "Jesus is A-Knockin'" and I was able to share the gospel in between the songs. The audience sang along with us, heard the message and gave us a standing ovation. God had answered my prayer.

8.   **Simple Preparation for Service** (Luke 9, 11): The Lord was a great leader who also believed in training leaders. In teaching and leadership, you first teach the disciple truth and principles. You exemplify it in your life. Then you send your disciples out to experience the lesson for themselves. This is what Jesus did for His disciples. He sent them out two by two with only the clothes on their backs. They were to preach the gospel, cast out demons and heal the sick. If they were accepted in a home, they were to stay there and minister. If not they were to wipe the dust off their feet and go on. This was the practice of prophets who brought the Word of God in the Old Testament. Wiping off their feet meant that they were left in the hands of God for His judgment. Jesus preached in Capernaum, Bethsaida, and Korazin. He said that because they did not accept his message they would not be inhabited. That was their judgment. Today these towns are just archeological relics.

Capernaum - ruins Synagogue

When the disciples came back they rejoiced because they had cast out demons and healed the sick. They performed miracles, but Jesus said not not to rejoice over these things but to rejoice that their names were written in heaven. The lesson for us is to live and minister in a simple way. Preach the message or give a testimony. Then let the Lord work. When we disciple others we can equip them, model the life and then send them out. We then gather for an evaluation or testimony time to share what God has done.

9. **Expect opposition**: In 2 Timothy 3:12 we read that all those who desire to live godly in Christ Jesus will suffer persecution. If we are living for God and obeying Him, we can expect this. The Lord told his disciples that they were called not only to believe in him but also to suffer for him. We get opposition from religious people who believe Jesus is accursed. Christians suffer in Muslim lands for preaching. They do not like the message.

Arabic letter for "Nasrani" (marked Christian home in Iraq)

When we go to Poland, we often experience opposition by priests. Sometimes the priests put on loud music as we preach the Gospel. One time a priest would not let us have a meeting in a public school. They really have no right to control it but they do have an influence. The Lord works out all things for his glory and our good. We decided to go outside and see what God would do. We started to play soccer and basketball with about 50 kids who were outside. After playing with them we decided to have a meeting with them outside. So, we preached the gospel and almost all of them made professions of faith.

10. **The Power of the Word** (Hebrews 4:12, John 3:3, Titus 3:5). The Bible tells us that faith comes by hearing, and hearing by the Word of God - Romans 10. The Holy Spirit using the Word convicts of sin, righteousness and judgement. It shows us our sinfulness. We are born of spirit and water. Water represents the Word of God. The Word converts the soul - Psalm 19. We are washed with the Word.

In Acts 1:8 Jesus promised the Spirit would come, and they would be His witnesses in Judea, Samaria and to the uttermost parts of the earth. The Holy Spirit emboldens and enables. When the disciples were under attack they started to pray and thanked the Lord for the privilege of suffering for their faith. They prayed for boldness to continue to preach.
The Lord answered as the place shook and they began to preach the Word of God with boldness. (Acts 4:31)

CHAPTER 12

PRAISE AND WORSHIP OF OUR GOD

One of the greatest conferences I have ever attended took place in Italy while we served there. Every other Christmas, the Christian workers from around the country would get together for a spiritual life conference. We have had speakers like Howard Hendricks, Stuart Brisco, and Haddon Robinson. When Ray and Ann Ortlund came, God really showed up. They brought us into the presence of God. Their theme was based on the book, *Lord Make My Life a Miracle*, written by Ray. They shared the three priorities of the Christian life.

Ray and Ann Ortlund

The first is our worship of God. The second is our love for one another as Christians and the third is our outreach to the world. We reach up to God, reach in to each other and reach out to others outside the faith.

During the conference we had times to really worship and adore the Lord. Then we had time to confess our sins to one another and encourage each other. We then made plans to do outreach.

A.W. Tozer

Worship is the most precious thing that we can do, but we have neglected it. A.W. Tozer writes about it in his article, "The Missing Jewel". Reaching God should be our number one priority.

We read in Psalm 22 that God dwells in the midst of the praise of his people. When we praise God, Satan is cast out, for he is allergic to praise.

In the revival under Hezekiah the King appointed priests and Levites to lead in worship (2 Chron. 29-31). They sang songs

and led the people. The Korean church is an example of a church that knows how to praise the lord. They praise and pray. Everyone brings a hymn book to church. They see the need. They have been under the Japanese, and communism. They know what it means to suffer and also how to praise the Lord in the midst of suffering.

PRIORITY OF Worship

We see the priority of praise in the formation of the camp of the nation of Israel in the desert. We read of this in Numbers 1 and 2. The tribes of Israel were to camp around the Tabernacle in a diamond shape with three tribes to the north of the tabernacle, three to the south, three to the east and three to the west. The tribe of Levi, however was to camp at the center of the oth-

Israeli Tribes camped around the Tabernacle

er tribes, surrounding the Tabernacle which was in the middle of the whole camp. The Levites were to be in charge of worship. So, worship was to be at the heart of the camp.

Jesus also taught the importance of praise. In John 15 He said we should abide in Christ and remain in His love. If we do this, we will obey His command to love one another. The first priority is to abide in Christ. When we worship we abide. In his high priestly prayer, Jesus first glorifies the Father (worships Him). He then prays for the unity of his disciples, and then prays that they can have an influence on the world.

The first half of the Lord's Prayer has to do with worshipping God. It says "Our father who art in heaven, hallowed be Your name, Your kingdom come, Your will be done on earth as it is in heaven." Following this there is petition for ourselves, that God would meet our physical needs, forgive our sins and lead us not into temptation.

In Jesus' rebuke to Martha who wanted Mary to come help her, Jesus said that Mary had chosen the better thing. Mary was worshipping the Lord and sitting at His feet.

In Acts 13, we find the church at Antioch. It was an international church with five gifted leaders. Paul and Barnabas were its founders. It was comprised of Jews and Gentiles. As they were worshipping, the Lord called out Paul and Barnabas for the work of preaching the gospel.

Place of Worship
People often make the mistake that they must be in some "house of worship" in order to approach God or pray.

In Jerusalem people go down to the Western Wall or *"Kotel"* to pray. The Muslims pray in the mosques and Christians visit their churches to pray. Because of this, Jerusalem is often called the city of prayer.

They say that when you are praying in Jerusalem it is a local call, not long distance.

Jesus made a revolutionary statement in John 4 in his encounter with the Samaritan woman. She spoke of worshipping God in Samaria and not in Jerusalem. Jesus said that it did not make a difference. Those who worship, "must worship in spirit and in truth."

Perspective of Worship
Our perspective on worship should always be God centered. We look to the Lord. Psalm 27 says: "The one thing I have desired is to dwell in the house of the Lord to behold the beauty of the Lord." When King Jehoshaphat faced an attacking army, the first thing he did was to organize a choir to sing praises to the Lord. In His prayer He stated, "My eyes are fixed on you, Lord. Paul says in Philippians 3, "But one thing I do, forgetting what lies behind I press on toward the goal for the high calling of God in Christ Jesus our Lord." As we run the race of faith, let us put aside the sin that entangles and keep on eyes on Jesus the author and perfecter of our faith."

Person of Worship

Who is the almighty God that we worship? Revelation 4 and 5 give us a rich and enduring description. John received a vision of heaven and the throne of God. Around the throne of God there were 24 elders seated on thrones. He also saw four living creatures which had six wings. These creatures were proclaiming, "Holy, holy, holy is the Lord God Almighty, who was, and is, and is to come." They cast their crowns before the throne.

In chapter 5 he sees the Lion of the tribe of Judah who has triumphed. He then sees a slaughtered lamb. We worship the Lion of Judah, the powerful and almighty one, and the Lamb, innocent and suffering for us all as a sacrifice. Our attitudes should be one of confidence, admiration and fascination.

Pursuit of Worship

Our pursuit should always be the Lord. We seek Him, we follow Him, and we thirst after Him. Paul said that he left everything behind to pursue the high calling of God in Christ Jesus. (Philippians 3) We are to run the race of faith, keeping our eyes on Jesus, the author and perfecter of the faith, who for the joy set before him endured the pain and has sat down at the right hand of God the Father. (Hebrews 12:1, 2)

Dwight L. Moody, the great preacher, once heard a man named Harley say, "It is amazing what God can do with a man who is totally committed to him. Moody said to himself, "I will be that man." He totally followed the Lord and God blessed him.

18 year old Moody

Prerequisites of Worship

There are certain prerequisites for true worship. We must have clean hands and holy hearts. We read in I Timothy 2 that men must lift up holy hands to the Lord. The Psalmist declares, "If I regard iniquity in my heart the Lord will not hear." Psalm 66:18. Revelation 4 and 5 teach us that surrender and giving God the glory are two prerequisites for effective worship. In chapter 4, the 24 leaders fell down before the Lord who sits on the throne and worshipped him. They lay their crowns before the Lord. They declare, "You are worthy, our Lord and God, to receive glory and honor and power." In chapter 5:8 the 24 elders again fall down before the Lamb. John heard the angels proclaiming, "To Him who sits on the throne and to the Lamb be praise and honor and glory and power, for ever and ever!"

Perpetuity of Worship

I will bless the Lord at all times: His praise shall continually be in my mouth ~ Psalm 34:1

Worship is to be a continuous activity. We must not cease to worship. The Psalmist says, "I will bless the Lord at all times; His praise shall continually be in my mouth." Psalm 34:1. Psalm 57:7 proclaims, "My heart is steadfast...." It is fixed on God. Paul declares in Philippians 4:6, 7 that we are not to be anxious but that by prayer and supplication with thanksgiving we are to cast our worries on Him and the Lord will give us His peace.

Panorama of Worship

The Scriptures teach that all of creation will worship God. That includes, man, nature, angels. Psalm 19 says that the wonder of the heavens, the skies, and the sun declare the glory of God all over the world. Their voice is heard in every language. Psalma 148-150 speak of all creation including the fish and animals that will glorify God and worship Him.

In Luke 19:40 Jesus says that even the stones would cry out in worship if no one else did. We've already seen that angels worship God. In Isaiah 6, the prophet had a vision of God who is on the throne, high and lifted up. He saw the angels proclaiming, "Holy, Holy, Holy is the Lord Almighty."

Power of Worship

What is the power of worship? When we worship God, what does God do? He gives victory. In 2 Chronicles 20 we read of King Jehoshaphat who was under attack by the Ammonites. The Lord spoke to Him to organize the choirs to sing. They sang and praised the Lord and as they did so, the Lord set ambushes against the enemy and they destroyed each other. The Lord won the battle.

In Acts 2, three thousand were baptized after the preaching of Peter. Then the Bible says that all these believers devoted themselves to the apostles' teaching, to fellowship, to communion and to prayer. They continued to praise the Lord and had favor with the people and the Lord kept adding to the church. Worship is powerful.

We also see the power of worshipping God in Acts 13. The church of Antioch was ministering to the Lord. There was prayer and praise. The Holy Spirit then broke through and spoke to them to send out Barnabas and Paul to preach the Gospel around the region.

When Paul and Silas were in prison in Acts 16, they began a praise party. They did not complain about their horrid conditions but sang praises to God, Who delivered them. The Philippian jailor was shocked and asked what he must do to be saved. He and his family were saved and God used them to start the church in Philippi.

I have heard of an instance in India when a group of Christians were attacked by Hindus. As they began to sing praise songs, God delivered them. There is another story about a bull that attacked a group of Christians. They sang and proclaimed the power of Christ and the bull was stopped.

Performance of Worship

In our own lives, God uses praise to develop our character. We have physical and mental health because of praise. Praise also helps us to decentralize self which is good for unity and prosperity in our families and our churches.

Panoply of Praise

There are many ways in which we can worship the Lord.
We worship with our tongues (Heb. 13). We worship by doing
good deeds (Heb. 13). We worship as we evangelize and
present souls to the Lord. (Romans 15). Giving to the Lord is
also a way of praising Him. We are tempted to be lovers of money (1 Timothy 6). Paul told the Ephesian
elders not to live for gold or silver.
It is more blessed to give. Silver and gold
have I none Acts 3:6. Jesus is worth it all.
In his book, *A Savior Worth Having*, E. V. Hill
writes of the worth of the name of Jesus.
He shares about where he buys his suits - at
the Jewish row in Chicago - and pays $100
for a suit that sells at Neiman Marcus for
$400. He says that if you are going to buy
clothing, you should buy something worth

having. When you pick a wife, you must choose one worth having. "Jesus," he says, "is a Savior worth having."

When I think of money I think of three things. We must live
responsibly, simply and generously. We must live responsibly.
Matthew 6:33 says we are to seek first the kingdom of God and
His righteousness. Everything we need will be added to us.
We must do the will of God. And according to 2 Thessalonians 3,
if a person will not work he must not eat. We must work.

I remember working at the Prudential Company one summer. Sometimes after lunch
break I would hide in a room and take a
snooze hidden under some cardboard.
This was thievery. I stole from the company.
When I became a believer, my work habits
changed. As I began to see work as a stewardship for the Lord
I worked hard.

We must also live simply. In Luke 10, the Lord sent out his followers two by two. They were to carry with them only those things that were necessary. In essence they were to carry things that would provide for them for one day. They were not to worry about the next day.

We are told to be content with food and clothing - Philippians 4, Proverbs 30:8.9; Hebrews 13.
One day, when they told John Wesley that his house had been burned down he said, "O well, that is one less thing to worry about."

We must also live generously. We must give. Honor the Lord from your wealth and your barns will be filled. (Proverbs 3).
In Malachi 3, we are told that if we tithe the Lord will, "open the floodgates of heaven and pour out so much blessing that you will not have room enough for it."

Head louse

Our daughter, Libby, experienced this personally. When she was a senior in high school we got lice. It was horrible. Because we were travelling during this time it took us a long time to get rid of them. Libby was especially distraught by the situation. One day she said to us that she knew why we had lice. While having her devotions she read a verse that said, "You are infested because you have withheld your tithes and offerings from Me." (Mal. 3:18-20)
She learned a great lesson from this experience and has seen God richly bless her financially as she obeys Him in this area.

We are told in 2 Corinthians 8:8, 9 and in Luke 6 that we are to give generously from the heart. When we obey God, He will give back. C.T. Studd was the best athlete in England who earned a lot of money. When he got married he decided to give all their wedding money away except $25,000. When he told his wife about his actions, he said, "Didn't the Lord say to give it all? Let us start marriage with nothing."

"'Funds are low again, hallelujah! That means God trusts us and is willing to leave His reputation in our hands.'
- C.T. Studd"

During my seminary days I was in an accident and I received about $6,000 from Workman's Compensation. I decided to give 20% of the money to the Lord. With the rest I took a trip to Israel, and bought an engagement ring for my wife. Then, when my car died my father gave me his car worth $7,000. This taught me that we cannot out-give God. On another occasion when visiting a church I felt the Lord leading me to give $100 in the offering even though I had very little money.

1,000 $
one thousand

At the end of the service someone came up to me and gave me a check for $1,000. Amazing!

QUOTES ON PRAYER

- "Prayer is not a check request asking for things from God. It is a deposit slip – a way of depositing God's character into our bankrupt souls."
  Dutch Sheets
- "There is a mighty lot of difference between saying prayers and praying." John G. Lake
- "Any concern too small to be turned into a prayer is too small to be made into a burden." Corrie Ten Boom
- "Prayer is not a discourse. It is a form of life, the life with God. That is why it is not confined to the moment of verbal statement." Jacques Ellul
- "In prayer it is better to have a heart without words than words without a heart." John Bunyan
- "Prayer is not so much an act as it is an attitude – an attitude of dependency, dependency upon God." Arthur Pink
- "There is not in the world a kind of life more sweet and delightful that that of a continual conversation with God." Brother Lawrence
- "Learn to worship God as the God who does wonders, who wishes to prove in you that He can do something supernatural and divine." Andrew Murray

CHAPTER 13

PRAYER - THE GREATEST FORCE ON EARTH

We come now to the last principle of revival. It is the great force of prayer. In his book, *Till Armaged-don,* Billy Graham shares about the situation in Israel during the time of Hezekiah the King. Sennacherib, the Assyrian leader boasted that he would annihilate the people of God and

Assyrian Rabshakeh insulting the God of Israel

possess the land. He stated, "Who of all the gods of these nations that my fathers destroyed has been able to save his people from me? How then can your god deliver you from my hand?" (2 Chronicles 32:14).

Assyria had built a vast and formidable war machine which ran ruthlessly over the nations of Judah and Israel. In the arms race of their day, they were definitely ahead. They subdued people and conquered countries. People trembled when Sennacherib spoke.

This reminds me of Isis who has threatened, murdered, and con-quered thousands of people in Syria and Iraq. The whole world is in fear of them. I have met their victims in northern Iraq (Kurdistan). One man related to me how Isis beat him severely and murdered his brother.

Hezekiah realized that humanly speaking no one could stop the Assyrians. They were superior in arms and manpower. The King knew that without a divine intervention all would be lost. He trusted in God and prayer was his secret weapon.

The Bible says, "King Hezekiah and the prophet Isaiah son of Amoz cried out in prayer to heaven about this" (2 Chron. 32:30). Here we have a king and a prophet of God, on their knees. God worked a miracle.

We read "And the Lord sent an angel, who annihilated all the fighting men and the leaders and officers in the camp of the Assyrian king. So he (Sennacherib) withdrew to his own land in disgrace.... so the Lord saved Hezekiah and the people of Jerusalem from the hand of Sennacherib king of Assyria and from the hand of all others. He took care of them on every side" (2 Chronicles 32:21,22). His word speaks to us today.

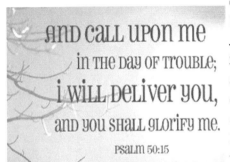

and call upon me in the day of trouble; i will Deliver you, and you shall glorify me.

Psalm 50:15

Isaiah and King Hezekiah made a great prayer team. It reminds me of the many times when Billy Graham prayed with our presidents.
And, when Menachem Begin (one of Israel's presidents) needed help, he did not consult the parliament but called Jerry Falwell.

Jerry Falwell   Menachem Begin

Isaiah and King Hezekiah prayed prophetically. I believe that

Jonah in Nineveh

they were praying not only for protection against the Assyrians but also that God would bless the Assyrians.
God wanted the Assyrians to be saved. He sent Jonah to them to peach the message of repentance and faith.
In Isaiah 19, we read of a future alliance between Assyria, Egypt and Israel. There will be a highway of blessings from Assyria to Egypt through Israel. And, today, God is saving many among the Syrians, Iraqis and Kurds.

During my first trip to Iraq, I witnessed the hand of God and his love for the Iraqi people. We were in a coffee shop in the Christian area of Erbil, the capital of Kurdistan. As we were enjoying our conversation with a fellow Christian worker, a man stood up to leave. My colleague then offered him a Bible. He said thank you and then stated that it was interesting that he was offered the Word. He said that he was a physicist who had studied at the University of Manchester in England. My colleague was also from Manchester. He said that he worked in the nuclear program of Sadam Hussein. He said that he was a Kurd (actually he stated he was Assyrian) who had lived in Baghdad for many years. He related that his house had been bombed and that is why he was living in Kurdistan now.

Kurdish Bible

He told us that he had been interested in the Bible since the day he was in Vienna for a meeting of the Atomic Energy Commission. He stayed in a hotel and found a Gideon Bible in the drawers. He began to read it.

He was delighted to receive the Word in his own language. The story does not stop here. This man began to study the Bible with our Christian worker friend. God showed his love for the people of this land.

The prayer of Hezekiah and Isaiah had a prophetic significance that is being fulfilled today.

Purpose of Prayer

The purpose of prayer is first and foremost a way to have fellowship with God. To have fellowship there must be a two- way conversation. God speaks to us through his Word, and we speak to Him through prayer. This is how we maintain fellowship with him.

The second purpose of prayer is to get things from God. We are told to call on the Lord and see Him answer, which is what Jeremiah 33:3 says. It says, "Call to me and I will answer you and tell you great and mighty things that you do not know".

This verse became very meaningful to me in a crisis situation. I was in Austria and was burdened about a problem with a very critical church member. As I was walking out of my apartment complex, I was calling on the Lord and claiming Jeremiah 33:3. I asked the Lord, "Please give me an answer!"

Immediately I got a phone call from an elder from another church. Their church was experiencing much the same thing from a woman who was formerly in our church. She had been a constant critic while she was in our church and a great discouragement to me. The elder related that she was also constantly criticizing their pastor as she had me. In fact, his pastor was on the verge of a nervous breakdown.

"We paid off the sanctuary. Wanne shoot for a new educational wing?"

Although I was sorry for this pastor, it encouraged me to know others were experiencing the same bitter trial. This gave me confidence in regard to the other member I was praying about because she also had an attitude problem. I knew that God would take care of her as well.

There is a third purpose for praying. I am indebted to the book *Destined for the Throne* by Paul Billheimer.

He believes that the main purpose of praying is to prepare the saints to reign with Christ. God is preparing a companion for Christ. We are his bride. We are betrothed to him. We wait for the consummation of this marriage at the wedding feast of the Lamb described in Revelation 19. He says that our faith is really a royal romance not a religion or just a relationship.

The fact is that we will reign with Christ. In 1 Corinthians 6, it is says that we will judge the world. In 2 Timothy 2:12, we read that if we suffer with him we will reign with him. In Revelation 2:26 it says that if we overcome we shall have authority over the nations.

And in Revelation 3:31 it says that he who overcomes will sit with Christ on the throne. Our apprenticeship for our future role is prayer. This is where we learn to overcome.

We have authority. In Luke 10:19, Jesus sent out his disciples. They healed, preached, and cast out demons. Jesus said to them that He had seen Satan fall from heaven and that He had given the disciples authority over Satan. In Matthew 16:18 Christ said He would build His church and that the gates of hell would not prevail again it.

Praying in the Upper Room

Priority of Prayer

Prayer is our priority. It must precede our preaching. When Jesus gave us his commandment and promise in Acts 1:8, He said the apostles would receive power and would be witnesses for Him. They began to pray. It lasted ten days. There were ten days of praying that preceded one day of power as the Holy Spirit fell upon the church in Acts. 2.

When the early church preached Jesus they were attacked. The first thing they did was to go back to the Father and pray for new boldness. In Acts 6 a problem arose with the church. The Greek speaking widows were complaining that they were being overlooked. The apostles immediately appointed deacons to take care of the problem. They said they should give themselves to prayer and then to the ministry of the Word. And the church flourished.

Before choosing His disciples, the Lord spent an evening in prayer, and in Matthew 9, the Lord said to pray the lord of the harvest to send forth laborers to the harvest. Pray first for laborers.

Pattern for Prayer

The Lord's Prayer has been prayed in churches throughout the world since the beginning of Christianity. In Jerusalem there is a special church which commemorates this prayer. The prayer is written on the walls in most of the languages of the world. Jesus taught this prayer as he was speaking on the Mount of Beatitudes as it is known today. In Matthew 6 Jesus spoke about the hypocrisy of the Pharisees who prayed in the open to be seen by men. They also prayed long and beautiful prayers so as to be admired by men. He encouraged his disciples to pray in secret so as not to be seen by men.

Greek Lord's Prayer

He then taught them to pray in the manner of the Lord's Prayer or Disciples' prayer as it could be called.

In this prayer we find a definite pattern. It starts off with worship, then a prayer for God's kingdom to come and then a prayer for our needs. It ends up glorifying God. He first acknowledged God as Father who is near us and has pity on us. A few years ago I heard the story of when Queen Elizabeth visit-ed Williamsburg, Virginia. She was taken around to visit the historic buildings and exhibits manned by hosts who were dressed in colonial garb. As she entered one building, an Afro-American host greeted the queen with a big hug. Of course, the British queen was shocked. This was not the English way. The newspapers had a great story. As they interviewed the affectionate host, she was quoted as saying, "I just wanted to show the Queen how much I appreciated her." The Queen who had first been a little bit flabbergasted by this emotional gesture, later recovered, and invited the gracious host to visit her in England.

Dear God,
Thank you for loving me
unconditionally.

We come to God first as our Father who seeks to embrace us with his everlasting arms. Our Lord is also in heaven. He is sovereign and king. He is also to be revered as holy. Hallowed be your name. We then have a prayer for God's kingdom purpose. His kingdom is to come and his will is to be done. To pray that his kingdom will come is to seek God's spiritual interest before our physical needs. There is a story of Larry Lea who had a physical problem. He went to a pastor and asked him to pray for him. The pastor laid his hands on him and then began to pray for God's church to be built. He prayed for people to be saved in China, and in the Middle East. "Pastor! What are you doing?" Larry burst out. "I need prayer for my health!" The pastor said we must first pray for God's kingdom interests and then for our physical needs.

So, first worship and kingdom prayer then prayer for our needs. "Give us this day our daily bread." God wants us to bring Him our needs! He ends the prayer with, "For thine is the power and the glory for ever and ever amen."

Pathos of Prayer
Pathos is the intense feeling or anguish of prayer. Prayer must be done in a passionate way. We read about Jesus in Hebrews 5:7, "During the days of Jesus life on earth, he offered up prayers and petitions with loud cries and tears to the one who could save him from death, and he was heard because of his reverent submission." Prayer and tears go together.

William Booth was asked how one could win souls. "Try tears," he answered. Jesus wept over the city of Jerusalem. "Oh how I wanted to gather you as a hen gathers its little chicks, but you were unwilling." (Matthew 23:37). In Ezekiel 9 we read of those who receive a mark. It is not the mark of the beast. It is the mark that is put on the forehead of those who grieve and lament over all the detestable things that are done in the city of Jerusalem. When Jesus was in the garden of Gethsemane, he prayed and drops of blood poured from his forehead. This is the true pathos of prayer.

Precise Points of Prayer

What are the things we are to pray for? Of course we know the example of Solomon. He asked for wisdom, not riches, power, or glory. God gave him wisdom to rule. We are encouraged in the book of Proverbs to seek after wisdom. Proverbs 3:5, 6 says, "Trust in the Lord with all your heart and do not learn on your own understanding, in all your ways acknowledge Him and he will direct your path."

We are to pray for the souls of men. In Matthew 9 we are to pray the Lord of the Harvest to send out workers into the harvest. When we preach the gospel we must pray for boldness (Ephesians 6). We must pray that our message will be clear and that God will give us opportunities.

We must catch the vision for reaching souls. While in seminary I met with a group of students who were praying for two things; they were praying for wives and to be used of God to reach the world. I saw the Lord answer. First, He led me to my beautiful wife, and then I praise God that he used us to help plant a church and do open air evangelism. The vision did not stop there.

The Lord gave my family the privilege of attending a wonderful conference in Europe. It was called "Love Europe." The theme of loving Europe captured my thoughts and imagination. The vision was to love Europe by reaching the cities of Europe, reaching into Eastern Europe, and reaching Muslims who were coming into Europe. God burdened my heart. This was before the Berlin Wall fell. In fact, we prayed for the wall to come down. We sang "Shine Jesus Shine," a wonderful song about making Jesus shine around the world. We were living in Milan, Italy at the time

which was in the center of Western Europe. In the providence of God, after the fall of the iron curtain, the Lord moved us to Vienna where I became the pastor of Grace Church and continued my

Open Air Campaigners

work with Open Air Campaigners. While there we started Reach the City campaigns in Vienna and in Eastern Europe. These campaigns were evangelistic in nature and helped share God's love for Europe. God opened up doors to reach many Muslims who had immigrated to Vienna.

We befriended them and saw God work. We baptized 80 Irani-
an Muslims who came to our church seeking to receive Christ.
They were disillusioned with the Islam espoused by the Mullahs
in Iran. I look back on our time in Europe as a fulfillment of the
vision God gave us through Love Europe.

While living in Europe we were involved in aggressive open air
work in the center of the city near St. Stephens Cathedral. Every
Sunday evening we did
sketch board evange-
lism. What a wonderful
opportunity. During that
time the war in Serbia
broke out. Kosovo was
the scene of a great
war. The Americans
bombed Serbia to pro-

tect the Muslims in Kosovo. This caused the many Serbians in
Vienna to begin anti American demonstrations on Sunday eve-
nings. And, where did they hold their demonstrations? In front
of St. Stephen's, of course, right where we did our preaching.
We continued our open air meetings, however, and one evening
as I was preaching the gospel one of the organizers of the
demonstration called me a CIA agent. A man threw down the
sketch board and pushed me. I tried to continue but could not.
The next week I did not feel like going. I thought I would stay

home with my family, eat pizza,
and watch a movie. But then, as
I was reading Jeremiah 1 the Lord
spoke to me. He said not to be
afraid of those who would attack
me, He would be with me and no
one could stand against me.
I said, "Ok, Lord, I'm going."

The same thing happened week after week. One week my good friend Phil Willer, an evangelist from England, was with me. As we were preparing I told Phil about my experiences. He suggested that if it happened again we should stop and help them set up for their demonstration. So, we did. We helped them set up chairs. The man who always attacked me came up, shook my hand, and said he was sorry for what he had done. Our loving ministry had melted his heart. We pray that the message we were preaching touched his life.

Of course, God wants us to pray for our needs. Give us this day our daily bread. Romans 8:32 says, "He who did not spare His Son but delivered Him up for us all, will He not also with Him, freely give us all things." In Philippians 4:19 we read, "And my God shall supply your needs...," not necessarily our wants. We have need of food, clothing, and loving protection. God is able.

MY GOD SHALL SUPPLY ALL YOUR NEED ACCORDING TO HIS RICHES IN GLORY BY CHRIST JESUS.

PHILIPPIANS 4:19

Persistence of Prayer

When we talk of persistence in prayer, we mean prayer that perseveres in spite of difficult hardships. Prayer is work. It is a struggle. It is one of our offensive weapons in spiritual warfare. Satan opposes saints who praise God and intercede. In the Sermon on the Mount Jesus said, "Ask and it shall be given, seek and you shall find, knock and the door will be opened." (Matthew 7).

Years ago an elderly lady in New Jersey began to pray for a local high school. She prayed that many from that high school would be saved and called of God to preach the gospel around the world.

In particular, she prayed for a young man named George Verwer, a young teenager who was into many worldly things. She sent him a Gospel of John.

One day he was in NYC and passed by Madison Garden where Billy Graham was preaching. He went in to ridicule the people, but God had other plans. On hearing the Gospel he fell under conviction and went

George Verwer

forward to receive Christ. God then worked in his life and he led many of his classmates to the Lord.

He went on to study at Moody Bible Institute and led teams on mission trips to Mexico. Eventually, he later was used of God to found Operation Mobilization, an organization that sends thousands of missionaries around the world. God answered the persistent prayer of this woman of God.

George Verwer

OM Operation Mobilization

Power Through Prayer

Ephesians 3:20 says, "Now to him who is able to do more than we ask or think according to the power that lies within us...."

God moves in the hearts of people. An example of Spurgeon's quote is found in the story of Moses who held up his hands in prayer as Joshua prevailed on the battle field. We all know this story.

Prayer is the slender nerve that moves the muscle of omnipotence.

Charles H. Spurgeon

meetville.com

When he got tired Aaron and Hur helped him. Prayer was related to victory on the battle ground.

Christ said we would receive power when the Holy Spirit would come upon us and we would be witnesses in Jerusalem, Judea and Samaria and to the uttermost parts of the earth. The apostles were filled with the Holy Spirit and began to proclaim the bold message of the kingdom from Jerusalem and beyond.

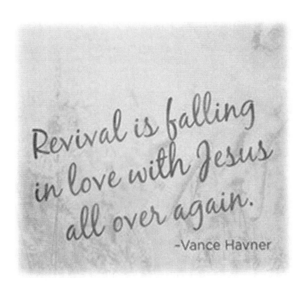

Revival is falling in love with Jesus all over again.

-Vance Havner

CHAPTER 14

CONCLUSION

This vital message has been burning in my heart for two years. I have preached it several times and in many places, including the USA, India, Israel, England, and Poland. The response has been the same all over: "We need this message in our land!" My burden is to take this message around the world. Of course, I need to preach it to myself and ask the Lord to start in my life. Revival starts at home.

My particular focus now is on the Middle East. In Israel, God has given us the privilege of working with both Jews and Arabs. We try to be peacemakers. The Lord has called me into a unique ministry: I work both as pastor of the Jerusalem Baptist Church and as a representative for the Fellowship of Christian Athletes. Being pastor of a  church has given me a home base for worldwide ministry. It has kept me in the Word and close to people. It has taught me the power of agape love. It has brought me into fellowship with other pastors of different denominations. We all have one goal: to see revival in our churches and our Land and to preach the glorious Gospel of Jesus Christ. Our church constantly prays for the unity of the Body of Christ in the Land.

"Soon and very soon, we are going to see the King!"

Being a representative for the Fellowship of Christian Athletes has put me in contact with the outside world. Sports are a way of bringing people together on the same "playing field".
It is said that the largest people group in the world is sports people. We have enjoyed working with Israelis in the American football league where we have teams comprised of both Jews and Arabs.

We also work with Palestinians organizing youth sport camps and teaching basketball, volleyball, and soccer skills.

Of course, we give spiritual input, teach the Bible and share the Lord. Many have made professions of faith.

Football training with Hoss Johnson

THE FCA VALUES

In our sport ministry we emphasize four principles that apply to sports and to life in general. They include integrity, the pursuit of excellence, servanthood, and team work.

114

Of course, whether in sports, business, or life, the need is for men and women who have a passion for God and communicate that passion to others.
That is what revival is all about.

"Lord revive our hearts
and may they overflow
with the love of God for others"

Your attitude toward Scripture can reveal your attitude toward the Savior. When your passion for God's Word runs high, your passion for God does as well.

Dillon Burroughs

meetville.com

- "God never gives us discernment in order that we may criticize, but that we may intercede."
- Oswald Chambers
- "The supreme thing is worship. The attitude of worship is the attitude of a subject bent before the King... The fundamental thought is that of prostration, of bowing down." Campbell Morgan
- Learn to worship God as the God who does wonders, who wishes to prove in you that He can do something supernatural and divine." Andrew Murray
- "All I know is that when I pray, coincidences happen; and when I don't pray, they don't happen." Dan Hayes
- "An unschooled man who knows how to meditate upon the Lord has learned far more than the man with the highest education who does not know how to meditate." Charles Stanley
- "Worship is a way of gladly reflecting back to God the radiance of His worth." - John Piper (Desiring God)

"Oh, lord my God—
when I in awe
and wonder
... "

QUOTES ON REVIVAL

- "Revival is not just evangelism, excitement, or emotionalism. It is the extraordinary movement of the Holy Spirit!" Del Fehsenfeld Jr.
- "Revival is not the discovery of some new truth. It's the rediscovery of the grand old truth of God's power in and through the Cross." Sammy Tippit
- "Perhaps the greatest barrier to revival on a large scale is the fact that we are too interested in a great display. We want an exhibition; God is looking for a man who will throw himself entirely on God. Whenever self-effort, self-glory, self-seeking or self-promotion enters into the work of revival, then God leaves us to ourselves." Ted Rendall
- "God loves with a great love the man whose heart is bursting with a passion for the IMPOSSIBLE." William Booth

"They tell me a Revival is only Temporary;
so is a bath, but it does you good!"
Billy Sunday

- "The spiritual disciplines of 2 Chronicles 7:14 are not just conditions for a true revival; they are the revival itself!" Lewis Drummond
- "We often have a tinted view of revival as a time of glory and joy and swelling numbers queuing to enter the churches. That is only part of the story. Before the glory and joy, there is conviction; and that begins with the people of God. There are tears of godly sorrow. There are wrongs to put right, secret things...to be thrown out, and bad relationships, hidden for years, to be repaired openly. If we are not prepared for this, we had better not pray for revival." Brian Edwards
- "Revival awakens in our hearts an increased awareness of the presence of God, a new love for God, a new hatred for sin, and a hunger for His Word." Del Fehsenfeld Jr.

Revival begins by Christians getting right first and then spills over into the world.
Charles H. Spurgeon
meetville.com

Contact information

Fellowship of Christian Athletes

Jerusalem Sports
8701 Leeds Rd
Kansas City, MO 64129 USA

Website: www.fca.org

JERUSALEM BAPTIST CHURCH

4 Narkis Street, Jerusalem
P.O. Box 154, Jerusalem, Israel
Sunday Worship at 10:45 A.M.

Email: jerbapch@netvision.net.il or jerbapch@gmail.com

 Jerusalem Baptist Church in Jerusalem, Israel

Website: www.jerusalembaptistchurch.org

The purpose of JBC is

to serve the interest of Jesus Christ in this city

until He returns.